Bridging the Gap

Between You and Your Folks

Written by: Patience Normoyle

Bridging the Gap Between You and Your Folks

Scripture taken from the New King James Version®. Copyright © 1982 by Thomas Nelson. Used by permission. All rights reserved. All emphasis added.

Cover and Layout: Patience Normoyle

Cover Pictures: Curtesy of Fotosearch and Getty Images

Initial Illustrations: Patience, Luke, and Nate Normoyle

Final Illustrations: Donald Staddon

Edits: Stephanie Hills and Kayla Mellas

Please Note: Some stories have been changed to protect the identity of the contributor.

If you find any errors in the book, please let me know. Improvement is always a good thing! If you want to write me for another reason as well, feel free to contact me at youandyourfolks@gmail.com.

ISBN-13: 978-1535409353

ISBN-10: 1535409355

Dedicated To You, the Reader:

May the love of Christ reign in your heart as you continue to learn how to love your parents in a selfless and Christ-centered manner.

Disclaimer:

Advice in this book is not meant as an "answer" for anyone. It is simply the author's attempt to encourage the reader.

Table of Contents

I Am So Grateful...

For the Lord Jesus: Thank you for being with me every step of the way. I really appreciate how You've taught me to walk with You. Also, thank you for reminding me to pray for others and bringing back to mind what writing this book has really been all about – growing closer to You.

For my parents: Thank you for loving me and teaching me to love the Lord. Also, thank you for being good examples, helping me set important disciplines in my life, and patiently showing me how to live my life for God. You both have taught me almost everything I have written about in this book. Thank you, Mama, for reading my chapters, pointing out poor sentences and helping me take out information that wasn't needed. Thank you, Dad, for your support and help with the content of this book. Also, thank you both for being there to talk to when I needed good advice. I love you both so much!

For my siblings: Grace, TaliJoy, Tabor, Luke, and Nate. Thank you for being such wonderful, encouraging friends. Thank you, Grace and TaliJoy, for being around to talk and helping me learn to spend time doing important relationship-centered activities. Thank you, TaliJoy, for reading my manuscript, telling me what didn't make sense, and helping me fix that. Also, thank you for helping me write "The Makeshift Memorial" story that is at the beginning and end of the book. That was such a *huge* blessing! Thank you, Luke, for taking my pictures for the book! Thank you Tabor, Luke, and Nate for supporting me, helping me with the illustrations, and being so much fun to be around. I love you all!

For Sarah and Grace Mally and all those in the BRIGHT Lights office who talked with me or prayed for me as I worked on this book. It was such a blessing and encouragement to have your prayers behind me! Thank you also for pouring yourselves into the BRIGHT Lights ministry. It has been a blessing both to me and to the girls I know.

For Carlos Bongianni and family, Joshua and Charlyn Woolley, Esther, James, and Donald Staddon and family, the Burgee family, Hannah Stelzl, Alissa Christiansen, Anna Weaver, Satu Nelson, James Brewster, Kate Ryan, Abigail Reeves, Jessica Neely, Stephanie Hills, Kayla Mellas, and everyone who read my document, talked with me, and offered advice, encouragement, and prayers as I moved forward.

For all those who helped me answer questions online on the blog while I was in the beginning stages of writing. Thank you for your time and valuable thoughts!

A Note from the Author

So, why do you think I decided to write this book? Was it because of my perfect childhood or, perhaps, my impeccable character? I wish. My story has many failures in it. Some of you reading this may be more qualified to write this book than I am, but I know that God's grace is sufficient—that's why I can put this book into your hands with confidence. I know that neither you, me, nor our parents are perfect. However, we know someone who is. God is perfect and will be the one to make a significant difference in our lives. So, I implore you to seek Him and make His will the top priority of your life.

I have definitely had times in my life when my relationship with my parents has been less than great. There have been times when enjoying each other in happy bliss seemed impossible. I have cried over our relationship, sought counsel over it, asked for prayer for it, and worked hard for it. I know my parents have worked hard, too—but still, we haven't found the elusive key to relational perfection. I'm convinced it's hidden in some mountain cave far, far away near the end of the earth. One day, if I have enough money and time, maybe I'll go search for it and bring it back for us all. Even though I haven't found the key, I am blessed to say that my parents and I enjoy an imperfect, yet sweetly wonderful, relationship. Funnily enough, it seems as if the imperfections in life and within ourselves have a way of helping us grow more mature and closer to each other as we view the imperfections as opportunities to grow.

I have learned a lot about imperfections. Through my struggles with pride, I eventually found out that it's not always a good idea to point out ways I think my parents could be doing better in parenting or some other area (this tends to be offensive). I have also noticed that they have pet peeves that I can steer clear of so we all can have a happier day. Speaking up has been another struggle for me. When I couldn't be understood, I had to learn to speak a little louder or more clearly. But, I had to learn to do so graciously, without allowing my emotions to become ruffled. That's probably been one of my biggest struggles, personally, because it has gone on for years upon years upon years, which has been tiring and strenuous. I have a naturally soft voice, so I have to kick myself in order to produce more hearable tones sometimes (especially when I'm tired).

Overall, my biggest, baddest, and most brutal enemy to my relationship with my parents has been selfishness. Sitting back and wishing for things to be done for me while I'm not willing to do the same for others. Allowing my emotions to run wild before exercising common sense. Basically: me, me, me, me. My self-centered mindset not only turned people off, but it also made it hard for me to develop the sweetness of relationship we all long for.

Manners are a huge part of thinking of others. Simple things such as not interrupting, being respectful to those in a room before saying something upon entrance, good table manners, saying please, thank you, and excuse me, and being all around kind have gone a long way for me. And do you know how I learned all this? From listening to my parents. "Patience, you are running past me and nearly bumping into me like I don't even exist. It would be more polite to slow down when you are walking by others in tight spaces." Instead of moaning an annoyed "okay," I have learned to smile and thank my parents for their advice and perhaps even reflect on why I appreciate it. "You're right, I am not being very thoughtful. I really appreciate that you let me know. I'm sure your advice will help others feel more respected by me in the future."

All of these stories should come together to answer my initial question: why did I write this book? Because I have found that many young people are missing out on the joy God intends for them to have in their relationship with their parents. This may be due to many things, one of which may be that they're not working on it. This relationship may be difficult, but it's sweet. It may be trying, but it's so worth it. Plus, there are so many more benefits to a good relationship than a bad one! A relationship will only be as good as you choose to make it. My prayer for each of you is that you will find a place in your hearts to nurture a Christ-centered love for your parents. I pray that you'll allow that same love to teach you to die to yourself and to lead you to a relationship that is special, loving, and altogether priceless.

Left to right: Nate, Patience, Luke, Michele (mother), Robert (father), Grace, Tabor, and TaliJoy

Introduction

Now at age twenty, the world considers me an adult. Nevertheless, I will remain a "child" for the rest of my life. I am a child of my Heavenly Father and a child to my earthly parents. Even after my parents die, I will still be called "Robert and Michele's daughter."

I am not an authority on this topic of relationships, but, like all of you, am learning more about how to love my parents. Jesus is the authority here and I hope to point you all to Him! I am praying for you—that God would help you follow Him in this area of honor and respect for parents. I would appreciate your prayers as well!

Did you know that there is only one command in the Bible in which the word "children" and a command are specifically tied together? That command is to honor your parents.

In Ephesians 6:1, children are admonished to obey their parents in the Lord, because it is right. According to Strong's Concordance, the word "obey" here implies a child being under their parents as one of less authority, listening attentively to them, and putting together steps of action when they're asked to change.

Biblically, a child's responsibility is obedience and honor. The goal in our relationship with our parents should be to live and speak in a way that honors them and live in a way that *brings them joy*. This whole honor thing is good practice for us. Ultimately, we desire to bring honor and glory to our Heavenly Father (1 Tim. 1:17). As we practice honoring our earthly parents whom we *can* see, it will become easier to honor our Heavenly Father whom we *cannot* see (1 Jn. 4:20).

What do you want to do with your life? In every area of life, whatever we choose to do, we will be under some sort of authority- whether God or man. Think of your relationship with your parents now as training ground for obedience to God later. How will we learn to obey the Lord, listen to His instruction, and respect the authorities God places in our lives if we never learn to do the same with our parents first? It is possible to learn these things later, but it would take more effort. It is best to learn how to grow in the Lord and how to honor our parents while we are young.

You're about to embark on an amazing journey. It might be uphill and it might bring some tears. But, be encouraged. Your sincere efforts will bear good fruit!

God put *them* in charge! What should I do?

"...reproofs of instruction are the way of life."
Proverbs 6:23b

"Mom, I am home!" Sue yelled through the house after school one rainy day.

"Sue," her mother sharply responded, "Don't yell through the house, and take off those filthy shoes! You are going to get my clean floor dirty again."

"Yeah, yeah. You clean the floor *every* day and are always so concerned about it. Give me a break... The Jones' always wear their shoes through the house and their mom doesn't get after them. What's the big deal?"

"First of all, we are not the Jones'," her mother remarked. "We are the Martins. Secondly, have you been through the house recently? There's dirt everywhere! Now, take off your shoes and stop talking back to me."

"Okay, yeah, sure..." Sue mumbled angrily as she took off her shoes and stomped off to her room to complain. "When will this ever end...? My parents will never change. They must not love me. They never have time for me and all they do is yell at me. Urrrgg... The Jones kids have *great* parents who actually let them do stuff. I wish I could go to the mall with Kelly Jones and the girls this Saturday, but Mom and Dad said no. I don't see why I shouldn't go! They always say no to everything I want to do. I can never do anything fun. I guess I will call Kelly and just let her know I can't go with them."

Ringggg. Ringggg.

"Hi Kelly! This is Sue."

"Oh, hi, Sue... Did you ask your parents about this Saturday at the mall?"

"Yeah, I did. But they said no."

"Again?"

"Yeah... Obviously, they think kids shouldn't have any fun."

"Hmm... This will be the fifth time now. You have got to do something about this. You need to have some fun. Did they give you any reasons?"

"Yeah, they said I shouldn't go to the mall without adult supervision. They still think I am a kid... but I'm twelve now. I can take care of myself!"

"Oh... I see. I think having a parent along would ruin all the fun. We like to be independent. Hey! I've got an idea. You could just say that a friend of ours is going - Mary, she's 22 and she's going to the mall with us."

"But, is she?"

"Of course not! But, if someone of age were there, they would let you go, right?"

"Well, yeah, but... I don't know. That would be lying."

"Sure, but they just don't understand what a kid our age needs. You would just be doing them a big favor. Hey, Sue, I've got to go. See you Saturday, and don't chicken out!" After Kelly hung up the phone, Sue had a lot to think about.

"I don't know what to do about this...I guess it wouldn't hurt. But, I'm scared because I've never done anything like this before. Like Kelly said, though, I do need to have some fun. It's really ok." Sue lied to herself. "I'm doing my parents a big favor by helping them give me what I need."

(Note: See how she has to lie to herself before she could lie to her parents? She twisted the truth in her favor! Oh no!)

Running downstairs, Sue hollered "Hey Mom!! You know how Kelly invited me to go with her to the mall on Saturday and..."

"I already said no," her mom interrupted.

"Yeah, but our friend, Margret, is coming and she's, um...24. So, can I go? Please??" concluded Sue with pleading eyes.

"Who is this Margret? I have never heard you speak of her before. Where did you meet her?"

"Oh...um...Margret was, uh, a substitute teacher one time at our school. She is really nice. See? I will be supervised now. So, can I go??"

"Well, I guess so."

"Thanks, Mom!!"

Running up to her room, Sue thought, "That wasn't all that hard after all. I get to go - yippee!! I will call Kelly right now!"

Sue did go to the mall, but as the weeks went by, Sue's relationship with her parents became worse and worse. Not only did she continue being dishonest, but she also became bitter towards her parents' imperfections.

One day, Sue was sitting in her room contemplating this issue. She thought, "Our relationship is just going downhill. Maybe I should do something about it. My parents *really* need to change. Maybe they should go get some counseling or something. Or, maybe I should talk to them about the things I see they could do differently."

That evening at dinner Sue brought up their relationship and how she thought it could get better. She shared with her parents the negative things she'd seen in their lives and how she thought they could change to make family relationships better.

(Notice how she was shifting all the blame on her parents?)

Despite her seemingly good motives, their conversation quickly turned into an argument. Her parents got very upset with her, and then corrected her on almost everything imperfect in *her* life. That was a real bummer.

Lying in bed that night, Sue was really hurt by her parents' accusations. "It was all their fault. *They* make me act the way I do. How could they say those things to me? They're so mean!" she murmured over and over again.

Wiping tears from her eyes, Sue turned her head and noticed something. "Oh...what is that little white thing on my desk?" Jumping out of bed, Sue flipped on the lights and walked over to her desk. "Oh, it is a letter from Violet, my good friend!! Mom must have put it up here for me." Sue tore open the letter excitedly.

Violet had moved away last fall, but she and Sue had kept in touch. In Sue's last letter to Violet, she had explained the problems she was having with her parents, hoping for some sympathy and understanding on how caged and mistreated she felt. She knew Violet had problems too and could give her some pointers on how to deal with her parents. Sue was excited to see what Violet had to say:

Dearest Sue,

Sorry it has taken me a while to get back. I have been quite busy. I am sorry to hear about your trouble! I also struggle with my parents at times, as you well know! But, when we moved, we found this really great church and my Sunday school class is taught by a dear elderly lady we've nicknamed 'Grandma.' One day after Sunday school, she asked me to come to her home. I was thrilled! I'd heard that she makes the best cookies. You should have been there to try some. ☺

After some small talk, she pulled a Bible off the shelf and asked me if she could share some thoughts from her heart. I was ok with that, so she opened her worn Bible to a couple passages that taught that no matter what others do or say, we still have a responsibility to show them love. She also opened to Ephesians 6:1, which talks about obeying your parents. She told me that just as it is their responsibility to raise me, it is also my responsibility to obey and honor them. I was a little skeptical at first, and she could tell! She's such a funny lady. You would have to be there to see; she's just so funny! Anyway, she challenged me to one week of honoring my parents and invited me back for cookies next Sunday afternoon. How could I refuse?

That week was so hard for me, Sue! Wow. It took humility, effort, and a lot of hard work. But, the harder I tried at it, the more I realized that I really wanted to know and love my parents more. I hadn't really realized that before. At our next meeting, I talked with her and learned about how problems in my relationship with my parents are triggered by sins like pride, discontentment, and many other things.

Maybe you could try to honor your parents for just a week too, and see if it helps any. You also might want to try reading the Bible. (That's what Grandma told me.) It really helped. My relationship with my parents isn't up to par yet, but it is better! I have more to say, but I want to call and talk over the phone later.

Praying for you always,

Violet

"Wow..." Sue thought, "I certainly wasn't expecting that! I don't know if I like this new spiritual focus in Violet or not. But, anyway, I guess I could work on honoring my parents and taming my temper for a little bit. Just one week. Things certainly can't get much worse than they already are!"

(To do your own week of honor, see Appendix 1. This story is continued at the end of the last chapter.)

The Command with a Promise

In my life, I have known the principle of being under parental authority from a pretty young age. Even though I obey, I often don't take the time to realize in my heart the *greatness* of what parental authority does for me. The authority parents are given to exercise over me gives me freedom to do what God intends for me to do. Without this freedom, I miss out on all the wonderful things God may have in store for me if I would only honor and obey. In obeying my parents, I'm also obeying the God who loves me more than they ever could and who desires the best for me (Jer. 29:11). It was He who commanded:

Parental authority gives me freedom to do what God intends for me to do.

"Children, obey your parents in the Lord, for this is right. 'Honor your father and mother,' which is the first commandment with promise: 'that it may be well with you and you may live long on the earth.'" Ephesians 6:1-3

"In a lot of ways, obedience is like support. Our authorities have a vision and goal. They need team members to make these goals a reality. By asking you to do something, they are inviting you to be part of the grand purpose they are working toward. You have the power to enable them to accomplish it and share in the eternal reward. Imagine what an encouraging blessing and support it is to your authorities when you help them accomplish what they are called to do! What an incredible gift! As long as your authority's requests are godly, obeying them is obeying God and it is aligning yourself with what He wants to accomplish on earth. Keeping this bigger picture makes obedience a joy!"

- Esther

When I was young, I didn't like homework. Though my parents would ask me to do my schoolwork many times, I thought there were more important things to do, like playing with my sisters. So, sometimes I'd "forget" my work or "lose" tests. Other times, I would pretend I had done all my schoolwork when I really hadn't. Not only was this very wrong, but it also didn't help *me* at all.

Did you say you were looking for my math book, Mom? That's funny. Have you checked, eh hem, my desk or, um, my backpack?

My parents knew the importance of schoolwork. I didn't. They knew I would need to know how to multiply and build good sentences. I didn't. They even possessed the intuition to know that I might even _like_ school one day, which is now true. I didn't.

Soon, my obstinate ways caught up with me. I had to do work from weeks previous. I retook some tests and, in some cases, erased the poor work I had already done in workbooks to redo things I never studied! After I learned _that_ lesson, I plodded along like school was a burden I "might just as well bear."

Much later, it occurred to me that my school years are a season that I will not be able to have for all of my life. So, I applied myself to my work and did it well. Believe it or not, I started enjoying all my subjects because I discovered how to enjoy learning. Proverbs 24:4 says it well: "By knowledge the rooms are filled with all precious and pleasant riches."

Because I have followed my parents' instructions, I am much happier now and will remain grateful for their advice for my entire life. My season of disliking schoolwork showed me how listening to my parents' instruction and immediately putting it into action is a good idea. I learned it is best to take and apply instruction as early in life as possible. I know my story is a common one shared by many young people, but what has it taught us?

Hopefully, such lessons will open our eyes to how valuable instruction is, not only for the blessings of God's promises, but also for those whom we can bless by our obedience, like our parents. In every stage of life, we are given a choice – to obey or to disobey, to be content or to be discontent, to enjoy or to be miserable. We need to find contentment in every situation God has for us, being confident that God has a bigger plan than we could ever imagine.

"For I know the thoughts that I think toward you, says the Lord, thoughts of peace and not of evil, to give you a future and a hope." Jeremiah 29:11

Authority – Is it good?

Most young people want to be free from authority as soon as possible and don't believe staying under parental authority is a good thing. However, parental authority has many benefits. I have highlighted three important ones below:

Protection - Parents have excellent foresight and wisdom on how to live life because they've lived so many more years than we have. Our parents have experienced much of life already. Instead of reinventing the wheel, we can stand on their shoulders of wisdom. They know which mistakes should be avoided and we can listen to what they have to say.

"Wow, so we can skip some mistakes in life by listening?"

"Yeah, isn't it great?"

Not that we won't make any mistakes at all, but we can avoid a lot of them by listening to our parents. In the end, parents can protect us from making wrong choices that may affect our physical or spiritual well-being.

Counsel – Parents know their children better than anyone else in the whole world. Not only that, but they *love* their children more than anyone else does too! Parents make good counselors and friends, especially when a good relationship is in place. (Note: In later chapters, we will discuss strategies to heal broken child-parent relationships.)

Guidance – Parents can say "yes," "no," or "maybe" to their children. Their ability to place these boundaries helps their children make important life decisions. Sometimes, when a child asks about something, it takes parents a while to give answers because they need to think and pray about it. Remember, God is ultimately in control. "The king's (or parent's) heart is in the hand of the Lord, like the rivers of water; he turns it wherever He wishes" (Prov. 21:1). Those who honor their parents' guidance will receive God's blessing (see Eph. 6:2-3)!

My Parents' Funnel System

My parents have told my siblings and I over and over again that they make boundaries for our good. They explain it with the help of a funnel. We all start off at the bottom of the funnel, where the opening is the smallest. This signifies us being young and immature and needing tight boundaries so we can stay safe and learn how to live our lives in a responsible way. As we prove to our parents that we can handle freedom properly, they will allow us to have more. On the other hand, if we show that we cannot handle freedom wisely, we either do not move forward or are pulled back until we can show responsibility and have a stronger foundation for our lives. As we become adults, we learn to make some decisions on our own. The older and more mature we become, the wider the funnel gets until our parents will one day release us from it completely. Although one day my siblings and I will be out of our parents' "funnel," we won't be out having freebie days without authority. God is still our authority and has boundaries set for our entire lives.

Is everything going well?

If things are not going well between you and your parents, perhaps God is using your parents to point out an area you need to grow in. Are you honoring your parents? Ephesians 6 says that when we honor our parents, things will go well with us. The situations we're in shouldn't determine whether or not we honor them. God has commanded us to honor our parents no matter what.

When things are not going well, we are not able to change our parents, our circumstances, or anyone else around us. The only person we can change is ourselves, and that is best done through the Lord's help. Is there anything God can reveal to you that you need to change or work on? Have you prayed about it?

Choosing to Honor in Correction

Sometimes we dislike the way our parents discipline us because it makes us feel bad or it seems like they don't understand us. Hang in there! "...No chastening seems to be joyful for the present, but painful; nevertheless, afterward it yields the peaceable fruit of righteousness to those who have been trained by it" (Heb. 12:11).

While no rebuke is pleasant, the fruit of a rebuke has a much greater value than what our flesh would choose instead (Gal. 5:19-21). As Hebrews 12:11 says, discipline bears the fruit of righteousness for those who learn by it. This fruit will help us honor our parents.

God is our heavenly Father, and He tells us that those who love Him will do what He says (Jn. 14:15). Our parents feel the same way. When they are obeyed, they feel loved and respected. As we keep obeying, it builds trust, which grows into a good relationship. This obedience must be consistent, though. Those who only obey until they get what they want are being selfish and insincere. Selfishness and insincerity will break both a parent's heart and his or her trust.

"My son, *keep* your father's command, and *do not forsake* the law of your mother. *Bind them* continually upon your heart; *tie them* around your neck...when you sleep, they will keep you; and when you awake, they will speak with you. For *the commandment is a lamp*, and *the law a light*; reproofs of instruction are the way of life." Proverbs 6:20-23

That Which is Longed For

What are some things you want in life? Peace, happiness, trust, people to love? People don't want these things "just because." Deep in the heart of every human being, there is a yearning and longing to have these needs fulfilled. God put them there for a reason.

If God put them there, and if He made us, wouldn't He know how to direct us down the right paths for the fulfillment of those desires? Or, did He make us with gaping holes in our lives so we could just enjoy the emptiness? That doesn't sound quite right.

"I am the Lord your God...open your mouth wide, and I will fill it." Psalm 81:10

Jesus is ultimately all we want and desire. He is our joy (Ps. 16:11), our Helper (Jn. 14:16), our Refuge (Ps. 91:2), and our

Sustainer (Ps. 54:4). He gives us strength to serve Him (Isa. 40:29), ability to learn new things, peace that surpasses understanding (Phil. 4:6-7), and provides the very breath we breathe. He is **IT**. We will learn this either now or later. Hopefully, we will learn to value Him before we die because one day, at the sound of His Name, every knee will bow and every tongue will confess that Jesus is the Lord of Lords, to the glory of God the Father (Phil. 2:10).

Relationship is something for which every human being longs. We want to enjoy other people and we want other people to enjoy us. That is completely natural. Jesus is an excellent choice of friend, and pursuing Him is a worthwhile endeavor. In addition, our parents are some of the most important people in our lives. We want to have good relationships with them, but it's often harder than expected. Don't give up, though!

Why We Should Persevere

Some may feel, "Why should I keep trying at this relationship thing? I already knew that it was going to be difficult and, well, my parents are just *really* hard to get along with. In fact, they're so difficult you couldn't even begin to imagine. It's hard to explain. They're just constantly bugging me. It's so annoying. Neither of them *ever* let me do what I want. They're really negative too. I've even tried to make things right between us, and it hasn't really worked. I don't get why things aren't working out. That's just what I have to put up with."

So why keep trying? Simply put, it's because you need them and they need you. They need you to be proud of, to love, to talk to, and to watch as you grow into a wonderful God-fearing young person. They need the caring touch only you can offer, the joy of watching your talents develop, and the presence only you can provide. Without you, there would be a hole in your family, whether they communicate that to you or not. *You are very special.*

You need them for all the reasons mentioned in this chapter and more. You need people to call "Mom" and "Dad." You need the sheltering care and advice that only they can give. You need them to worry about you, to fuss over you, and be as annoying as you think they are. Sometimes, they lose words to express "I love you" and instead express it in all their worries and fusses. Give them grace.

Another reason to persevere is because God wants to show you His strength and love, especially in the hardest and most stressful situations! He needs *you* to give Him your life so He can prove to the world that His ways are best. As He tells us in Romans, His will is good, acceptable, and perfect. What could be better than something good, acceptable, and all-around perfect?

"And do not be conformed to this world, but be transformed by the renewing of your mind, *that you may prove what is that good and acceptable and perfect will of God.*" Romans 12:2

What to Expect from Humans? Not Much.

It's tempting to want to build our lives around certain people. We want to be like them, talk like them, dress like them, or maybe just look up to them. It's a good thing to look up to others. Godly role models are definitely encouraging. But, what happens when they fail? People often become disappointed when the friends or family members whom they have looked up to fail in some way. But, couldn't we all?

Many people build their life, security, and happiness around the love of their parents, a schedule, or some other thing. Then, one day, something happens and their world shatters to pieces. Other people build their life security around Christ and even when people fall (which may be painful for the time), they still stand secure upon the solid Rock of Ages.

You see, we *must* build our lives on the solid ground Christ offers us. All other ground is unstable and will wash away when storms pass through (Lk. 6:48-49). When we learn to rely on

We must build our lives on Christ.

God alone for our inner needs and fulfillment, we will be able to *give* more to our families and become more of a vessel filled with joy and love. Yes, we all still need each other (very, very much), but we also know that when people fail, the world has not ended. There is a constant peace in knowing that God never changes and is a faithfully-constant friend and provider. He is someone we can rely on because He is perfectly faithful (Deut. 7:9) and everything He promises comes to pass (Jos. 21:45).

We cannot place our expectations on people because people are imperfect. Don't expect anything from your parents! The less we expect of them, the more grateful we'll be when they do the nice things they do for us. Thus, the less we expect, the happier we'll become! Our parents might never change, but *we* can. We can learn, grow, and move forward. We need to expect to be disappointed by people, and likewise, expect to be upheld by Christ.

"Because You have been my help, therefore in the shadow of Your wings I will rejoice. My soul follows close behind You; *Your right hand upholds me.*" Psalm 63:7-8

Pursuing a Relationship

"The father of the righteous will greatly rejoice...let your father and your mother be glad, and let her who bore you rejoice." Proverbs 23:24-25

Susanne doesn't always feel close to her mom. In fact, sometimes she feels totally at odds with her. It's just hard to communicate sometimes. One day, Susanne and her mom were

in the kitchen cleaning together and Susanne thought it would be nice to be with her since they barely spend good, quality time together. However, as time wore on, it seemed like everything went wrong. Susanne misunderstood her mom and her mom misunderstood her. Susanne

ended up crying in her room and feeling discouraged about their relationship. What should she do?

How Hard Should We Try?

Is a relationship with my parents really something I should work on? What if my parents are unreasonable? What if they don't seem to want what is best for me? None of my friends work on theirs. Should I even bother?

Your relationship with your parents will probably be one of the most *special* relationships in your life, *given* you allow it to become that. Most likely, your parents love you and have cared for you more than anyone else you've ever known. Consequently, they have great intuition for counsel and advice in your life. And despite all the odds, they are your parents to love.

It's important for us to realize that relationships are never a recipe. There has never been a successful "Steps to Perfect Relationships" manual published. Jesus is the only Son who ever had a perfect relationship with His Heavenly Father. He is our example. We humans will always be in stages of growth and maturation, so don't put it on yourself or your parents to be perfect. Follow Jesus' example; no one will ever be there for you like the Lord will. Trust His hand in your life and He will provide you with strength for this journey.

"But those who wait on the Lord shall renew their strength; they shall mount up with wings like eagles, they shall run and not be weary, they shall walk and not faint." Isaiah 40:31

Thought Number One

"What if my parents don't want to spend quality time with me and I'm really not too thrilled about spending time with them either? What if they think of me as just another 'rebellious kid' and I think of them as 'strict parents?'"

When you think of a good relationship with your parents, what do you think about? Some people totally dismiss the thought of good relationships because they've never had a good relationship with their parents and they haven't really seen anyone else who has one either. In addition, a lot of young people have expectations about what their relationships should be like and judge their parents as incapable of such, forgetting that this relationship is just as much their own responsibility as it is their parents'.

"One piece of advice I would give to someone going through family difficulties is this: We are here to minister to others, not the other way around. Jesus called us to minister to others around us, including our family. When we go into difficulties with this attitude, it changes everything! We no longer expect anything but are there just to serve. When people see that you want to serve, that motivates them to want to serve too. All this leads to a better relationship with your family and Christ." –Layel

Misplaced Expectations

In my relationship with my mom and dad, I struggled with having expectations of them that they didn't know about. I thought they should do certain things, but I didn't let them know what I wanted. Silly, right? One of those areas was getting hugs. If I wanted a hug, I would just wish I could get one and watch in gloom if another sibling got a spontaneous hug. My parents had no idea that I wanted one, and if they had, they would have given it! Sadly, many daughters and sons don't ask for what they need or desire. Instead, they wish:

"I wish my parents would spend more time with me."

"I wish my parents would hug me more often."

"I wish my parents would express their love to me verbally."

"I wish my parents would talk to me more."

Many other wishes have been made and left unfulfilled simply because they have not been made known. When you do tell your parents your desires, be it through tears of repressed longing, and always lovingly and respectfully, they will most likely respond with something like, "Oh! I didn't know you were needing hugs! How can we help you get more in the future??"☺

One thing I hope I'm not conveying is the idea that you should ask you parents for every little thing you want and exhaust them in the effort! Here's a tip: if you see a gap where your relationship could be strengthened, let them know. If you start to realize you're asking or begging for the unnecessary, be forewarned: parents have needs too and they *can* get overwhelmed. It would help you to ask what their needs are as well.

If you want your parents to spend more time with you, let them know you desire to have more one-on-one time together. When you tell them this, ask them if you could plan a time to be together. This is something I had to learn, because my parents can't read my mind. But, they do care for me, and I can ask them for some of their time.

When you want or need something, it's important to put on an attitude of loving respect. Imagine how you would feel if you had a chance to ask a king for something you wanted. How would you word your request? You would probably be *very careful* to make *everything* sound as respectful as possible. In the same way, a loving, understanding, and respectful attitude will help your parents feel respected for their time and efforts! As a side note, your parents should never be able to guess when you want something because you put on a nice, polite attitude. Be happy and helpful all the time so they won't think you're trying to manipulate them with your good behavior.

Seeing and Meeting Needs

One way to make your parents feel loved is to look around and see how you can help them. My mother especially enjoys it when my siblings and I help her make dinner, wash dishes, or set the table. When my Dad gets home from work, we like to go outside to greet him and ask him what he wants help carrying in.

When I was 12 or so, I started noticing a tendency I had to become disappointed when my parents didn't do the things with me I wanted them to. I was struggling with Dad because his interests didn't match up with mine very much. Slowly but surely, I started to realize that Dad had a lot to do and was doing things for our families' benefit, such as fixing cars, working outside, or learning how to fix things around the house. I've learned to view spending time together with Dad under an old car as just as much fun as going out somewhere together. Both going out and hanging out under a car have one thing in common: a chance to be with and talk to the other person. Although doing what *I like* is fun, learning how to work together is fun too, because we're accomplishing something useful together.

It comes as a surprise to most, but these types of useful activities are actually quite nice. When two people are excited about meeting needs and serving others, work becomes fun and memories are made *left and right*! Meeting the needs of others is a good way to use quality time. Trying to meet personal needs as more important than the needs of others, however, usually ends up in sadness because of selfishness. Self is never fulfilled, but serving others is fulfilling!

Self is never fulfilled, but serving others is fulfilling.

I know someone who doesn't like spending time with their parents. "Why should I spend time with my parents if I know they are just going to cut me down the entire time?" What should a child do? Above all, know that Jesus sees the good in you and pray for the pain and unresolved hurts in your parents' lives. I know that's easier said than done, but keep going to Jesus in prayer and He will help you. He has promised (See Phil. 4:6-7, Jere. 29:11, Mat. 7:7-11, and Prov. 3:5-6).

Remember to seek the Lord's face in trials, and beware of times you think you need to point out your parents' weakness. This often backfires and causes a setback in building a good relationship (like in the story at the beginning of the book!). If you are feeling bitterness, anger, hurt, or hatred toward your parents, pray and ask God to take those nasty feelings away. It may be prudent to seek godly counsel to help you develop a heart of love and forgiveness for them. Most importantly, put your hope in Jesus, and not in your parents' progress.

I can't have a good relationship with my parents because they're always correcting me!

Parents are given to us for instruction and correction (Prov. 22:6), yet many children get annoyed by their parents' advice and boundaries (Heb. 12:11). Instead of getting upset with our parents, we really should learn to overflow with gratefulness because of their corrections. With practice, we will be more grateful towards our other authorities as well.

One of my friends shared how she likes to try to avoid correction as much as she can. This is good in that it keeps her from disobeying her parents. But, my friend had another perspective on this avoidance of correction. She sees how she is afraid of instruction instead of excited about it. She knows she should love hearing instruction and find joy in it because it can help her grow. Instructions can and should be treasured. That's how she wants to respond to them - as if they were a precious gift. However, she still struggles with stubbornness from time to time.

There was one instance of this that stands out in her mind. It was the day before a big test for a competition, and she was studying the material she thought would be important for the test very diligently. Then, her dad suggested it might be a good idea to focus her efforts on another part of the test material than what she had been studying for. My friend had a hard time accepting this advice because she already had her own "perfect plan" of how to study. What her dad had mentioned wasn't included in her scheduled study plan. Also, she didn't think what her dad had suggested to study was going to be on the test at all and that following his advice would be a waste of time.

So, she decided to go talk to her mom about it, and her mom said that it would be best do what her dad recommended. Reluctantly, she studied what he had advised. The next day at the test, she was completely shocked. What she had studied the night before was definitely on the test! If she hadn't study that part, she could have failed. When she recalls this story, she remembers that her parents have special wisdom she should always listen to.

After more discussion, she told me she has learned to liken learning to love instruction with learning to enjoy vegetables. People eat vegetables because they know vegetables are good for them. As shocking as it may seem, as people eat vegetables more often, they learn to like vegetables more! My friend is going to use this thought process to grow in a love for instruction. She is going to practice giving up her own way more often so that she can listen more to instruction and learn how good it is for her.

We should appreciate what our parents have to tell us. When we appreciate what people are saying, we tend to listen more attentively to it, and even apply it better. That's exactly what our parents want us to do. They want us to listen to them and apply what they're saying! When we learn to appreciate instruction, our parents will feel appreciated as well, and that will lead to a fonder relationship.

The Precious Treasure

This a riddle. What I'm thinking of is incomparably valuable. Those who find it think of it as they think of jewelry. It is considered to be like a treasure, and those who have it live longer and more peaceful lives. You grow wiser because of it and become more pleasing to God as a result. Have you guessed it yet? Yep! It's instruction!

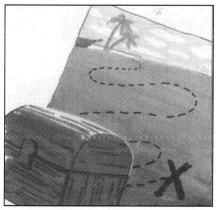

"My son, hear the instruction of your father, and do not forsake the law of your mother; *for they will be a graceful ornament on your head and chains about your neck.*" Proverbs 1:8-9

"My son, if you receive my words, and treasure my commands within you, so that you incline your ear to wisdom, and apply your heart to understanding...*if you seek her as silver and search for her as for hidden treasures*; then you will understand the fear of the Lord and find the knowledge of God." Proverbs 2:1-5

"My son, do not forget my law, but let your heart keep my commands; for *length of days and long life and peace* they will add to you." Proverbs 3:1-2

"My son, keep my words, and *treasure* my commands within you." Proverbs 7:1

"*For wisdom is better than rubies*, and all the things one may desire cannot be compared with her." Proverbs 8:11

I can't have a good relationship with my parents because they're not present in my life.

In special cases, it is not possible to have a good relationship with parents. Some parents are imprisoned, on drugs, or absent, silent, or deceased. In these situations, we still need to honor them in our conversations and by the way we live as much as possible, even though it's really hard. We can also pray for them. We should pray for their salvation and that God would be gracious and use the difficult things in their lives to draw them closer to Himself.

God gives us every season and trial in life for our benefit. He wants to be like a father to us and wants us to look up to Him for provision and protection, just like a child would look to an earthly father to have their need met. He simply wants a relationship with us.

"A father of the fatherless...is *God* in His holy habitation." Psalm 68:5

If we do have parents present in our life, our focus should not merely be to have a relationship with them, although that is important. Of greater importance is to pursue a relationship with the Lord. That way, even if the relationship with our parents doesn't turn out the way we imagined, the one with God will still grow, because God cannot fail us. Without Christ, we would be on our way to Hell. He went to great lengths to rescue us from that eternal suffering. Don't you think after all that effort He would want a relationship with us?

We need to be sure to pursue a relationship with the Lord even more than a relationship with our parents and others.

What is a friend?

Growing up, I wanted my parents to be more like "friends" to me. I wanted them to tell me less of what to do, how to do it, and when to do it and just put up with me the way I was. Have you ever felt that way? Now that I'm older, I'm actually glad my parents didn't try to be my "friends" in the way I wanted them to be. If they had been, they probably would have tried not to offend me. As a result, they wouldn't have corrected me hardly at all. If they had never corrected me, then I probably wouldn't know how to hold a nice conversation or even how to chew with my mouth closed!

Sometimes, the meaning of "friend" gets a bit too broad. Is a friend someone who gives you everything you want? Is a friend someone who takes you out to eat? Is a friend someone who plays with you? Is a friend someone who shares interests with you? All these things a friend may do, to some extent, but we need to know what a true friend is and *how to be that for our parents.* What is a true friend and what would that person be like? Read the verses below and think about what it means to be a friend. Remember that an authority friend will be different than a peer friend. Your parents will correct you, they will set boundaries for you, and expect obedience from you. Their training will be unpleasant at times, and you will have to choose how to respond. Prayerfully consider how to apply true Christ-like love to your relationship with your parents.

"A man who has friends must himself be friendly, but there is a friend who sticks closer than a brother." Proverbs 18:24

- In what ways can I be friendly toward my parents?

"Confess your trespasses to one another, and pray for one another, that you may be healed. The effective fervent prayer of a righteous man avails much." James 5:16

- Should I be more open with my parents?
- Is there anything I have hidden from them that they should know about?
- How can I pray more for my parents?

"Let us consider one another in order to stir up love and good works." Hebrews 10:24

- How can the way I live encourage my parents to follow Christ day-by-day?
- How can the way I show love to my parents encourage them as they love others?

"Be kindly affectionate to one another with brotherly love, in honor giving preference to one another." Romans 12:10

- What makes my parents feel loved?
- How can I put my parents' needs above my own?

"Beloved, let us love one another, for love is of God; and everyone who loves is born of God and knows God. He who does not love does not know God, for God is love. In this the love of God was manifested toward us, that God has sent His only begotten Son into the world, that we might live through Him. And this is love, not that we loved God, but that He loved us and sent His Son to be the propitiation for our sins. Beloved, if God so loved us, we also ought to love one another." 1 John 4:7-11

- What is love?
- Why should we love our parents?

"Children, obey your parents in all things, for this is well pleasing to the Lord." Colossians 3:20

- In what areas should I work on pleasing the Lord by obeying my parents?

Attempting to do these things for your parents will help bridge the gap that so often separates children from their parents. Remember, when you are working on a relationship with your parents, the goal is not to have them respond in the way you want them to, although that might be nice. Your ultimate goal should be to please the Lord and do what is right in His sight (Eph. 5:8-10).

What do your parents do to make you feel loved?

"I feel very loved when my parents compliment me with words of praise on my character or a task I have accomplished. This praise is always multiplied when they express it in front of other people. I also feel especially loved when they spend time talking with or listening to me." -Anna

"Wow, my parents have done so much out of love for me! They gave me life and raised me in the ways of the Lord! What a lot of trouble and huge expense! I am so grateful and forever indebted to them. Some ways they have shown love, far above what is necessary, are by going on trips as a family and by writing letters to me. It was special to get a call from Dad last week just to talk and hear how things were going." -Esther

"My parents make me feel loved by going out of their way to do something special for me, or by spending time helping me accomplish goals that I have. For me, it's probably more spending time together, working on projects, and things like that which make me feel loved and appreciated by my parents. Of course, there are other ways that I see their love and am so grateful, but it's during these times that I feel it most." –Bethany

Do you think your parents might feel loved when you do these similar things for them?

Fun Ways to Show Your Parents that You Care about Them

Effectively showing love to a parent will differ from parent to parent because everyone has a different way to feel loved. Even so, here are some ideas to get your thoughts started!

Answer the phone lovingly: When you know that your parents are calling in, say something sweet to make them feel special, like, "Hello, this is the happy daughter of Robert Normoyle! How may I help you?"

Practice spontaneous acts of kindness: Do something to relieve their burden when they don't know you're doing it. Listen for things they need done, such as the windows washed, the garage swept, or the trash taken out. Just washing or putting away dishes one night without being asked would be a blessing! Don't expect to be found out or look forward to praise or reward. Let the mere fact that you were able to be a blessing bless you in return.

Let the mere fact that you were able to be a blessing bless you in return.

Offer a shoulder massage: Ask your parents if they'd like a massage. Some people - Dads especially - *really* appreciate this!

Develop thoughtful habits: Some examples might be a hug and kiss before bed or a warm after-work hug and "Welcome home!" Other habits might include a simple and enthusiastic "please" and "thank you," or apologizing sincerely when you've wronged them.

Allow time for your parents to be alone: This might mean simply being quiet for them, cleaning something, making dinner, or being sure to get in bed on time. If you're old enough, you could even babysit so they can get out.

Give when they'd expect it least: Parents know that children like to give them gifts on Mother's Day or Christmas, but why not surprise them with a small gift "just because"? It could be a love note, a bouquet of wild-picked flowers, or even a picture you drew. It doesn't have to be big, and you can be as creative as you want. The point is to let them know that you care!

See Appendix One for more ideas on showing parents love.

Back to Susanne

Remember Susanne at the beginning of this chapter? She went to help her mother clean in the kitchen and then got discouraged about their relationship. After being discouraged and quietly crying over it in her room, she wiped her tears and prayed that God would help them communicate better next time. Since she was overwhelmed by all the ways she thought their relationship could grow, she asked God to help her in each area and give her strength to joyously seek improvement. Susanne wondered why she was having this struggle with her mom. Remembering that God has a purpose for every trial, she decided to try to be grateful. What she has learned throughout her life about gratefulness is that it doesn't come naturally for her. She must *decide* to be grateful. With this in mind, she pulled out a piece of paper and wrote: "Ways This Trial is a Blessing to Me" on the top of the page and underlined it. Next, she numbered the page one through five and wrote the following:

1. *I can learn to show genuine love to my mom.*
2. *I can trust God to be my rest and comfort and learn to be strong in His love when my mom doesn't understand me.*
3. *My mother can be blessed to see that I really want to have a good relationship with her as I keep praying for her and sweetly desiring her best.*
4. *Others who have these same trials can be encouraged by how I'm learning to rely on the Lord for strength.*
5. *I can learn valuable communication skills about responding to difficult situations graciously.*

Not long after she had jotted down the last thing on her gratefulness list, her mother called for her. "Susanne! Could you help me set the table for dinner?" Susanne's heart filled with dread. She didn't want to go downstairs, but she knew she had to. So, she responded respectfully to her mother, prayed a quick prayer, and ran downstairs to help. She knew that having an enjoyable time with her mom was a two-part deal, and that she was only responsible for one of those two parts – her part. With this in mind, she went downstairs with a desire to help her mom and remain sweet and kind, even in the face of difficulty.

Unfortunately, Susanne's mom was pressured and stressed out about getting everything done in a certain amount of time, but that didn't keep Susanne from responding well. She tried to be as cheery as possible and help wherever it was needed. It went pretty well at first, but after a while, Susanne started having some negative thoughts circle in her head. She wondered why her mom was being so cranky with everyone. She could think of quite a few things that could be going differently if only her mom would have a different attitude. After asking to be dismissed, she went to a bathroom, knelt by the tub with the door closed so no one could hear, and prayed:

"Lord, please bless my mother with faith in you. Don't let her be fearful of things that haven't happened yet, but help her to trust in you. Give her kindness for others who get in her way and help her to love others as you have loved her. Please give her a successful day today, Lord, and let her have joy in you, trusting in her heart that You have good plans for her."

After this, Susanne hurried back to the kitchen so she could help again. Blessing her mom with character and strength through prayer had helped give her a renewed outlook on the situation around her. It was hard for her to think any negative thoughts about her mom anymore because she had just sincerely asked God to bless her with what she was needing. After the business of the day slowed, Susanne wrote a little encouraging note to her mom, explaining how much she appreciated everything her mom did for her and listing the positive qualities she saw and appreciated in her.

That night, Susanne thought about everything that had happened. She remembered how difficult it was at first and how after she had prayed, God brought to mind things that she could do to help the situation go smoother. Grateful for how God had worked through her that day, she knelt again and thanked God for His goodness to her. Looking forward to what she was going to learn the next day, she crawled into bed and fell fast asleep.

Without God, I'm a Flop

"Abide in me, and I in you. As the branch cannot bear fruit of itself, unless it abides in the vine, neither can you, unless you abide in Me." John 15:4

If you didn't want your relationship with your parents to get better, you probably wouldn't be reading this book. Maybe you're having a hard time, or maybe you feel like your best efforts have been in vain. Maybe you feel ok with the relationships you have, but think they could improve a bit. If you can relate to any of these feelings, this chapter is for you.

So, You Feel Like a Flop

Your home is tense and your relationships fragile. You don't like being around your parents. You think it's their fault that things are going downhill and you can't wait until you're old enough so you can finally pack your bags and ditch the prison you've grown up in.

Well, you might not feel that bad, at least not all the time. Sometimes you really truly want to have better relationships with your mom and dad, but you don't know how to go about doing it. Your parents are easily offended by you, and you are easily offended by them. Will things ever get better?

Growing up, I would get easily offended by the tone of voice my parents used when they explained things to me. When their voice was raised, I didn't like it at all. I am sensitive and just don't like tense situations in general, but later I learned something that helped me. I learned *why* they raise their voice. I'm not justifying that yelling is always the right thing to do, I just want to help you understand *why* your parents might react the way they do so you can learn to love them through it all.

Why They Raise Their Voice

Why do your parents yell? Yes, they could be angry with you for something you have done, but chances are they're just scared. Maybe they're angry, but they're scared too! Scared <u>for you</u>! Your parents love you. They have held you in their arms, invested in you, cared for you, and sacrificed for you. When they see something going wrong in your life, their first instinct is probably fear. "What's going to happen?" "Is my child going to get hurt?" Sometimes this intense love is what comes out the most during those dreaded "loud conversations" (also known as arguments).

Maybe your parents are trying to help you understand that something you are doing (or are thinking of doing) is dangerous. They've lived longer than you have. Maybe they have some good advice, but instead of just telling you about it, they express themselves with a raised voice.

Do your parents feel like they have to yell to get you to listen? That could be another reason they are yelling. It would help us, as children, to consider our parents' point of view, ask them where they're coming from, and learn what their concerns are. Show interest in knowing what they want you to do and follow through with their requests. If they aren't interested in letting you know the "why" part of their request at the moment, simple obedience probably wouldn't hurt!

Sometimes people raise their voice or yell when they're stressed out. It may or may not be your fault that your parents are upset. But, your mature response to the situation would help either way. Why is your parent stressed out? Dinner's not on the table? Your sister is failing in school? Someone lost their job? *What can you do to help in these situations?*

Sometimes what is needed most is for you to simply pray. Pray that God would use the situation for His glory and your family's growth. Ask God to help you seek what would benefit His kingdom instead of just asking God for what you want to happen (Mat. 6:33). Pray and ask God to help you know how to serve your family.

You could serve by helping around the house, by trying to lovingly encourage your siblings to do the right things, or by simply enjoying the time you have with your family. Be aware of the needs around you. If there is a conversation going on in the room you're walking into, take note and don't

whistle or make a loud announcement. If someone yells at you, don't yell back! Sometimes changing something about your life or attitude can be helpful to making a relationship smoother. Try to understand what your parents are trying to communicate. In stressful situations, it's always nice to have grateful, kind, and thoughtful people around to make the home a happier place.

Relationship No-Nos

The following are some things that can harm your relationships. These things often become habits that occur without noticing during conversations with others.

Being negative: Negativity is a sure way to discourage yourself and those around you. Are you discouraging those in your house by using negative words? Ask God for creativity to find ways to encourage others. Use words that will put smiles on the faces of your parents and siblings. If you use any discouraging verbal expressions, stop using them! There's no need to discourage those around you, especially the parents who love and care for you.

Our goal should be to encourage others and build them up (1 Thes. 5:11). Specific discouraging or dishonoring words and expressions you might consider removing from your vocabulary are: "annoying," "stupid," "dumb," "Whaaaat?!?!," "Duh," "Huh?," etc.

Some of these words are only discouraging if used in a certain context. "What," for example, could be used encouragingly: "What!! I'm so amazed at how you bought me exactly what I wanted!", or discouragingly, "Whaat!?! I *always* clean the toilets." See the difference?

Arguing: This occurs when both parties think they are right and try to convince the other with their point of view. This often ends in hurt feelings and with no real winner. So, don't argue! Replace arguing with listening. Listen to what others have to say and be willing to contemplate their point of view. You may not like hearing this, but there is at least a 50% chance that the other arguer could be right.

Talking back: Talking back after receiving instruction insinuates that you know more than your parents do. It's like telling them what you think should and shouldn't be done, or saying they are wrong and you are right. It's very disrespectful and creates unnecessary tension. It might be good to ask your parents to point out when you're talking back and get their input on how to stop. Sometimes, the reason children talk back to their parents is that they don't understand what their parents are saying. However, talking back only makes things worse. If you don't understand what your parents are trying to tell you and you feel frustrated, take a deep breath, pray, and say as nicely as you possibly can, "I really want to obey you, but I don't understand what you are saying/why you are asking me to do this. Could you explain _____ to me." or "I know you will be making the final decision, but could I share an idea with you?"

Mean or grumpy expressions: Expressions communicate how you feel about a person. If you are going to have a good relationship with your parents, wouldn't it help if they knew you thought well of them? The way we express ourselves outwardly begins on the inside, so make sure that what you think about others is nice and proper! Abide in hope, not in that your parents will change, but that Christ will change *you.* Sometimes you might think, "Well, if they thought better of me, maybe I would start thinking better of them too." Remember what Jesus said: "Inasmuch as you did it to one of the least of these My brethren, you did it to Me" (Mat. 25:40). Would we treat God, our president, or a celebrity in the same way we treat our parents? Our parents can take the place of "least" in our hearts sometimes, even though they are such a special part of our lives. We need to be humble and treat them the way we would if Jesus was watching us every moment (Prov. 15:3).

Bad attitudes: Certain attitudes can communicate that we don't care about other people or their ideas. Sometimes just the way we say something can communicate a bad attitude. Bad attitudes can be portrayed in facial expressions, too, so watch out! Using a mirror or recording yourself might be helpful to practice a good attitude and to check yourself for an encouraging tone of voice and kind facial expressions. Encouraging facial expressions and a kind tone of voice will work for you in many areas of life, beyond your relationships with your parents. Almost everyone likes people who are encouraging!

Rockets and Obedience

In the Scriptures, we are commanded to obey our parents: "Children, obey your parents in the Lord, for this is right" (Eph. 6:1). There are many different types of "obedience," but only one is right. Let me explain. Children can "obey" with a grumpy attitude, they can "obey" with their tongue sticking out, and they can even "obey" a few hours after  they were asked to do something. However, those children are barely even obeying at all! Rockets illustrate obedience by their speediness. Slow rockets would be a strange sight. In fact, it would be a dangerous sight. If rockets didn't go fast enough, they'd crash and burn! In the same way, slow obedience is not good at all! Obedience is not true obedience unless it is immediate, yet thorough, and done with a good attitude.

Do you want to blow your parents off their feet and make their cheeks hurt from smiling too big? Here's an idea for practice. Try saying these things out loud: "Yes, ma'am (happy smile), I'd love to do that for you!", "Yes, sir (happy smile), I'd be happy to!", "Yes, ma'am (happy smile), anything for you, mother!", "Yes, sir (happy smile), whatever I can do to make your day better!", "Yes, ma'am (happy smile), I will do that right away!", "Yes, sir (happy smile), you can count on me to get the job well done!" Responding respectfully will help our parents know we love and appreciate them for who they are and for everything they do for us.

Relationship To-Dos

Make use of uplifting words. Amazing, spectacular, incredible, outstanding, fabulous...wow! What an encouraging family of words! "Mom, you did a spectacular job making dinner tonight! Thanks for your effort!!" "Dad, you are an incredible baseball player! Thanks for coming out to play with me!" How else can you make use of uplifting words in your life? Perhaps you could write a list of encouraging words on a piece of paper and place it somewhere you will see often so you can be reminded to use them. You can remember to use encouraging words every time you want to respond with a neutral and boring "ok" or "cool," or even as a way to be positive when you're feeling negative. Encouraging, sincere, and heartfelt compliments go a long way in helping people feel appreciated and loved.

Make certain words and expressions taboo. If you have any discouraging expressions, stop using them! There's no need to discourage those around you, especially the parents who love and care for you. Your goal should be to encourage others and build them up (1 Thes. 5:11). Discouraging or dishonoring words and expressions might be "annoying," "stupid," "dumb," "Whaaaat?!?!," "Duuh," "Huh?" etc. Discouraging thoughts can also be portrayed in facial expressions, so watch out!

Respond promptly. If mom calls, "Timmy!!", his response should be "Yes, Mom?" *immediately*. If you can, go to your parent when they call you so you can have eye contact with them as they speak. Even if you know *beyond a shadow of a doubt* that that particular call means that your mom is going to ask you to set the table for the fifth night in a row, go and help *joyfully* anyway. Your parents want to know that you're listening to them, that you care about them, and that what they have to say is important to you. Honor that! It's worth their relationship.

Ask good questions. When your parents are explaining something to you, don't just stand there and mumble "Uh huh, uh huh..." while twirling your hair. Ask questions to understand what they're saying and to show them you understand what you're being told. It might be good to say something like, "So, this is what I heard: you want me to mop the hallway, clean the toilets, and study for my test, right?" Other good questions to ask while your parents are giving instructions might be, "What time do you want this done by?" or "Is there anything else on your list?" Good questions are always respectful and never come out like, "Do I *have* to do that noooowww?" People come up with good questions when they're listening to the person talking and meanwhile planning how they can do what they're being told. After the task is carried out, it's always good to report back to your parents and let them know you're done. They will want to know how well you did it, too, so be prepared to give account! Also, ask permission to be excused from the task when you are done so you don't leave them feeling like you've only done the job half-way. This attitude of responsibility will help your parents feel respected and will help you know how to properly complete tasks.

Take note of their advice and wishes. Often children and parents experience tension over particular things. Perhaps it's the music you listen to, the friends you hang out with, the clothes you wear, or the movies you watch. Listen to your parents and make the changes necessary to honor them in full. If you want to go the extra mile, you can make them feel especially appreciated by asking them for advice on what you should wear, listen to,  or who you should hang out with, etc. Do you already know what they're going to say? Break the tension today and obey!

Smile: Make your parents feel loved and appreciated by smiling a big, award-winning, ear-to-ear, loving grin to make them feel special! Smiling can be more powerful than you think.

Listening to God

We will have days where our parents seem fussy, insensitive, and negative, but in the Ten Commandments, God gave the command, "Honor your father and your mother, that your days may be long upon the land which the Lord your God is giving you" (Ex. 20:12). That is not conditional. We are not supposed to only honor our father and mother when they are being nice to us! God wants us to honor them *all the time* no matter how they act. We are sinful humans just as they are, so we need to leave room for compassion in our hearts. In hard times, we can learn lessons about ourselves, about interacting with them, and about God's character. We need to show grace to them as God has shown grace to us.

Love is not only a feeling, but also a choice.

In my life, God used a sibling of mine to help me learn to love others better. A few years back, I was doing laundry with this sibling and he was being difficult. In my heart, I struggled with thoughts of negativity towards him. Thankfully, the Lord stepped in and gave me a much-needed reminder.

"Patience, you have sinned worse sins against me than this. It was your sin that put me on the cross. I have loved you with an everlasting love and forgiven you in *full*. <u>Love your sibling</u>."

God really caught me off guard there. *I was stunned.* How could I have been unmerciful to my brother in my heart after God had been so merciful to me? How could I forget to call on the Lord and show others His love after He has blessed me so much? God, in His mercy, saw *my need for mercy,* and in mercy, stepped in with a rebuke. God calls us to show mercy even to those who are rubbing hardest against us, because *we are all sinners in need of God's grace.*

"By this we know love, because He laid down His life for us. And we also ought to lay down our lives for the brethren."
1 John 3:16

"It can be very difficult to seek God's will in every moment of my day when He is not the first thing that comes to mind. I have found that meditating on a verse or verses throughout the day keeps Christ in the forefront of my mind. Then, when an issue or decision arises, my first thought is to seek His opinion. By the way, I find it easier to keep a Scripture verse or passage in my thinking if it is put to music. My mind recalls music faster than words and the music will continue to run through my head..."
-Anna

Teamwork

We often like to think of parent-child relationships as a two-way deal. True, it does take love and effort on both the parent's end and the child's end to make the relationship work out. However, God says that it's a three-sided deal when we rightly include Him. If we leave Him out, our lives would be miserable.

As children and parents work together with God, God wants parents to lead and children to honor and obey (1 Tim. 3:4, Eph. 6:1). In addition, God ultimately wants each of us to be in a relationship with Him.

"Behold, I stand at the door and knock. If anyone hears My voice and opens the door, I will come in to him and dine with him, and he with Me." Revelation 3:20

Listen to Jesus' knock and open the door. When allowed in, God's power and love can increase our efforts to love each other. We must rely on God and trust Him for the basic needs of family life. He is the One who can ultimately help us. He simply wants us to take each care to Him in prayer. Even if we do have fiery ordeals with our parents, God can replace the ash heaps in our lives with His beauty (Isa. 61:3).

Children and parents need to be rooted in Christ. As they stay connected to Him, their love for each other will grow. As life goes on, they will be able to advance in life, living for God's kingdom in God's strength. The triangle below shows how when God, parents, and children are all joined together, they can move onward in godly family life. As they all live connected to Christ and learn of Him through His Word, they move forward in life as families, advancing God's kingdom, and living for His glory.

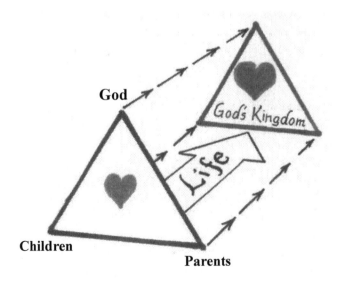

You might be thinking after reading the last paragraph, "Whoa! This book isn't for me! My parents are not that godly. I don't even know when they last read the Bible!"

With God all things are possible (Mrk. 10:27). And besides, this book isn't on how to raise your parents; it's about helping you learn to love and respect them! Pray for them and allow this book to encourage you to honor them no matter who they are or where they are in life. But as you do so, watch out. To quote from an audio presentation our family likes:

"Danger! Unavoidable turbulence mixed with unexpected showers of blessings ahead!"

–Lamplighter Theater

"Hey, do you have a minute?"

It has always been a huge blessing to me to have older, likeminded girls and ladies come alongside me to pray with as I walk through life. It's such an encouragement to have someone you can trust to share your heart with! Even though a parent can be that someone, others who aren't involved in everything your family is involved in day in and day out can often shed fresh light on things.

"Can I talk to you?" Maybe there's someone at your church to whom you could ask this question. Maybe it's your pastor or pastor's wife, an elderly person, or a vibrant young believer who can point you to Christ. Here are some things to look for:

- Someone who loves the Lord and is a strong Christian

- Someone who has a good relationship with their parents
- Someone of whom your parents would approve
- Someone you can trust
- Someone who won't condemn you
- Someone who won't take sides. (If someone sides with you, it could make it harder for you to see needs for growth in your life and could cause you to become bitter against your parents. You don't necessarily need someone who will "side" with your parents either, just someone who can help you see where they're coming from.)

How to Share with Others

Whatever you do, don't spread a bunch of bad information about your parents to other people! That's called gossiping. Share what is bothering you so it's off your chest, honor your parents for being your parents, and try try *try* to speak well of them. Share a struggle and pray. Share the struggle and ask someone you trust if they've ever had your kind of problem and if there was anything they could share that helped them through it. Talk about how to seek God through your struggle. Ask them for insights on how God could have you grow in this situation. Don't allow the person to go away feeling angry at your parents! As much as possible, spread good, encouraging, and kind words about your parents and, in general, about all of your authority figures. I'm sure you'd want them doing the same thing for you (Mat. 7:12).

"Let no corrupt word proceed out of your mouth, but what is good for necessary edification, that it may impart grace to the hearers." Ephesians 4:29

The Tent Story

Our family was preparing for an exciting trip with our friends to go camping in the Appalachian Mountains. We worked together to get things ready, and finally we were all itching to leave. The morning we left, we hopped in the car to begin our weekend adventure.

After we arrived at our destination, we set to work putting up our tents, only to realize that we had left the tent poles for our biggest tent at home, two-and-a-half hours away! How could we forget tent poles, of all things?

One of my sisters exclaimed, "Oh boy! I'm so glad we forgot the tent poles! Maybe we could sleep under the stars tonight! I love adventures!!"

Soon after, Daddy addressed my brother, "Tabor, do you have any rope in your survival pack?"

"I think so!" Tabor answered as he ran off for the van.

Soon after, Tabor came back with some small pieces of rope. "Humph," Dad thought aloud, "this won't be enough. Do we have any twine?"

Yes, our friends had brought some twine. So, we used the loops on our tent that would have originally been used for tent poles to pull twine through. We attached the rope and twine to the branches of two nearby trees. After that, it didn't take long to have the tent into a "tentish"-looking shape!

The ropes attached to the top of the tent made it impossible to put our tent cover on. When my sisters, friends, and I climbed into our sleeping bags that night, we all hoped that it wouldn't rain, that all the twine would stay intact, and that no bears would come attack us. Thankfully, nothing bad ever did happen, and we all had a decent night's rest.

So, I guess we could say we did an okay job of "roping up" the tent for that one night, but could you imagine trying to stay in it for multiple days, or maybe even a week? There's the threat of rain, rumor of bears, terrible cold, and uncertainty of structure. It was workable, but it was certainly not the best tent.

We will never be able to become all we are meant to be in God's plan unless He becomes the very backbone, or "tent poles," of our lives. We need to turn to Him and ask Him to uphold in us a life of strength, joy, and honor. When tested, will the tent poles of abiding in Christ keep you intact and radiant, or will the tent collapse pitifully on itself because you relied on weak supporting structures like rope or twine, which grow weary under much weight?

"When the whirlwind passes by, the wicked is no more, but *the righteous has an **everlasting foundation**.*" Proverbs 10:25

After returning home, we set up the tents on our back deck to rid them of any moisture before storing them. After sleeping in a "baggy" roped-up tent, it was amazing to see the tent with the poles in place again! Walking inside felt like being in a mansion compared to what we had slept in only hours before.

God gave us parents to help provide meaningful structure to our lives so we can be useful in the purposes for which He created us. Imagine how useful a tent would be if it rejected the structure the tent poles provided. Sure, it could get by without them (like we did), but it would not be protected from the elements, nor last as long, nor even look as nice as it would with the tent poles in place. Without poles, the tent was a flop. Without Christ and authorities as supporting structures in our lives, you and I would likely be flops, as well.

To learn more about this foundational relationship with Christ, see the Conclusion on page 215.

How Little Things Get Big

"He who is faithful in what is least is faithful also in much..." Luke 16:10a

Relationships are made of lots of little things piled together. These "little things" can be as tiny as a subtle attitude or even a thought. Did you know that *the way you think* impacts the relationship you have with your mom and dad? You don't have to say anything for an attitude to show.

Thoughts

"My Dad never does anything fun with me."

"My mom *always* tells me what to do."

"My parents never really show any love to me."

I have struggled with negative thoughts about my parents and have watched others have negative thoughts toward their parents as well. Often, when someone says or thinks something negative about another person, their goal is to feel better about themselves and/or make the other person look bad. But, when they elevate themselves by thinking or speaking badly of others, it doesn't turn out the way they think it will. It ends up making them look bad, and much worse that the other person they are being negative about. On the other hand, it is admirable when people pull through difficult situations with good things to say, even about people who have hurt them. Those types of people make others think, "Wow! I want to be like that."

Thoughts are a lot less obvious than words and actions, but they can impact a relationship. They are the revving engines behind our words and actions. Ultimately, we want to reach a place where we have built good habits into our thought lives. We should be mindful that God knows our thoughts very well, even before we think them (Ps. 139:2)! Imagine if your thoughts went up on a movie screen for others to see. What would people think? What would your parents think? Would your parents feel more or less loved when they see your thoughts? Keep in mind that even if people are not able to see your thoughts now, the Bible says, "For there is nothing...hidden that will not be known" (Lk. 12:2).

> Watch your thoughts...they become words.
>
> Watch your words...they become actions.
>
> Watch your actions...they become habits.
>
> Watch your habits...they shape your life.
>   Anonymous

Our thoughts are what tick our clocks. We must make sure they are positive, loving, and Christ-honoring. If we know a certain thought isn't the best, we need to "take it captive," and make it obey Christ. Make your thought obedient to Christ so that you can be a true follower of Jesus, even in your thought life.

"...bringing every thought into captivity to the obedience of Christ." 2 Corinthians 10:5b

Honor in the Heart

One day, after shopping with my mother, we were packing up the car and some bad attitudes erupted that made the trip go less smoothly than we had anticipated. As small comments started to build up, I allowed negative thoughts and feelings toward my mother and brother irritate me.

When we got home, Mama commented on how well I had handled myself. It had gotten difficult between the three of us. As she said these things, my mind wandered back to what was happening inside me during that situation. If I had really *truly* handled the situation well, I would have been thinking <u>good things</u> about Mother the *entire* time.

In this particular situation, I can think of a number of things I could have done differently in my thought life:

- Praised the Lord for a chance to develop character (Jas. 1:2-4)
- Asked God to help me put myself in Mama's shoes and understand her better
- Prayed for understanding and compassion
- Developed joy as I practiced thinking on things that are true, noble, just, pure, lovely, of good report, and praiseworthy (Phil. 4:8)
- Prayed for those people involved who were having an equally hard or harder time than I was

If I had continued to believe negative things about Mama, our communication would have been impacted. Reliving and rethinking negative things about a person is called bitterness, something we want to cast *far away* from ourselves (Heb. 12:14-15). By catching myself while the situation was still in play, I was able to stop and turn away from bitterness, asking God to help me do better next time. Catching our bad thoughts before they become bad habits is a good way to aim for better relationships.

Dishonoring Obedience

All too often, young people are tempted to believe that obedience and honor only relate to our actions. We think that if we follow through with what our parents say to do, then we've obeyed them. Believe me, this is not the only ingredient of true, honoring obedience. You can "obey" your parents without having any real honor for their authority at all. For example, have you ever given an angry "yes, ma'am" after a rebuke from your parents? The "yes, ma'am" part of it was honoring, but the attitude was not.

A godly woman who we'll call Rachel was once counseling a young girl who outwardly acted like an angel. However, after talking to her for a while, Rachel found out why the girl was behaving so well. The girl told her that she knew if she acted nice and did everything her parents said, then she could get what she wanted. Rachel counseled her against this attitude, but the girl didn't listen.

Later on in her life, this girl was not able to get what she wanted from her parents, despite all her hard work to be good. She got mad at her parents and ran away from home. The girl's attitude was neither one of love for her parents nor of love for the Lord. She wanted everything to go *her way*, and if things did not go the way she wanted, she would erupt and rebel. She may have been obeying outwardly, but she did not have an obedient heart.

We shouldn't think things we would not say out loud, because "out of the abundance of the heart [the] mouth speaks" (Lk. 6:45). Even good words can bring out a stinky attitude because of stinky thoughts. In order to honor our parents, we have to love them, work with them, and trust them. We have to proactively do our utmost to *think the best about them and what they want us to do.*

When we find ourselves being corrected, it is easy to see the faults of the person rebuking us, and as a result, not benefit from their advice. Putting ourselves in our parents' shoes, we can better understand why they get concerned about certain things in our lives. We need to be glad that they love us enough to point out things like that! Even when it seems like they are being 99% unreasonable, we still need to seek first God's kingdom and His righteousness (Mat. 6:33). In other words, we need to ask God what He wants us to learn from the situation. Our parents are commanded to train us, not to please us; it's their responsibility from the Lord (Prov. 22:6).

At times, their training will seem unpleasant to us, but since our parents are responsible for training us, why not try to make their job a little easier?

It is up to us to surrender ourselves to the Spirit of God, swallow our feelings of pride, and submit to our parents, even though they are imperfect. Many times, when I try to understand where my parents are coming from and why they are saying what they are saying or doing what they doing, I actually end up agreeing with them and realizing that I was wrong to begin with! It's always good to know when you're wrong. *Humility* is the key to accepting a rebuke and being able to enjoy its peaceful fruit of righteousness.

Thoughts are very powerful. Proverbs 23:7 says "For as he thinks in his heart, so is he..." What we think about our relationships can determine what they become.

Let's say, for example, that you believe that you never have any fun with your parents. Perhaps this belief is based on a circumstance or hardship you have experienced in the past.

Because of a negative belief you have about your parents, your heart becomes hardened, and the next time your parents do something nice or spend time with you, you don't see the blessing. Instead, you seem to be able to find all the things that are wrong about the nice things they do! If you had recognized the negative thought about never having any fun with your parents in the first place and replaced it with something positive, you could have actually enjoyed the time with your parents instead! See, I'm giving you all advice on how to have fun.

When I go to God, He helps me see that He put my parents in my life for a good reason. He shows me that if I don't submit to them, I won't be submitting to God in my heart, in my thoughts, or with my life - all of which Christ deserves for what He did to save me. Often, when I sense a tension or a struggle between my parents and I, I go to the Lord and pray. When I honestly reflect on the issue at hand, I usually find the same issues that I have with my parents between myself and God. Sometimes I'll be able to realize that I'd been prideful and communicated that I thought better than they did.

Is there a particular struggle with your parents that mirrors your relationship with the Lord? Could God feel the same way about you as your parents do? Oftentimes, God, in His faithfulness, gives us real-life situations so He can show us spiritual lack of character!

I'd like to challenge you to pray and think:

- What are the things the Lord might have me change in my life, attitudes, or schedule that do not honor my parents?
- Are there struggles between my parents and I right now?

- Is there something my parents get after me for (such as not listening) that the Lord could hold against me as well?
- How can I let the Lord work through me to be a blessing in their lives?
- How can God be glorified through my relationship with my parents?

Blind Spots

Have you ever noticed how some people don't see their own bad habits, but how easy it is for others to see them? In the same way, we're often blind to weaknesses in ourselves that others can readily see. It's much easier for us to see when other people are sinning than when we sin ourselves. That's one reason it's so important to stay humble and listen to advice!

Parents are people who can tell us where we need to grow. This is a huge blessing because most people are afraid to point those things out; perhaps because they don't want us to get upset at them! But still, we need to hear when we are wrong, and parents are willing to help us with that. Parents love us enough to point out things that could potentially harm us or others if we keep doing them. They help us see our faults and give us pointers on life.

Your parents may be trying to think of a good way to help you grow and mature in a certain area of life right now. Wouldn't it be neat if you were to ask them how you could change at the same time they were praying or thinking about how to tell you about that area you need to change in? That would be refreshing both to you and to them, wouldn't it be?

Asking questions like this is very meaningful. When asked in sincerity, such questions go a long way in making parents feel loved and honored. Hearing the question, "In what ways can I honor you?" will bring a precious joy to their heart. So, be encouraged, as it is a great thing to do!

Some might be thinking, "But, I don't want to ask my parents those questions because if I do, I'll have to change!"

This fear is understandable. I get scared sometimes too! If there are things in our lives that will have to change after asking that question, it is natural to be afraid of how they will respond. Regardless, there is joy and freedom in having a clear conscience, which may lead to a closer relationship.

Note: If you feel that your parents are unapproachable with words, do acts of kindness for them with no expectation of returned favors. *See Appendix 1 and 2 for ideas on this.*

I should add that sometimes there may be an issue that neither you nor your parents can put a finger on. In those times, it is *paramount* to take the issue to the Lord and pray something like, "Lord, thank you so much for my parents and for all the ways they have been a blessing to me. I would like a stronger relationship with them, and with you as well. Could you please open my eyes to see my weaknesses and help me exchange them for Your strength? Also, help me to grow strong in character so that I can be a blessing both to them and to You. Thank you! Amen."

"Be anxious for nothing, but in everything by prayer and supplication, with thanksgiving, let your requests be made known to God; and the peace of God, which surpasses all understanding, will guard your hearts and minds through Christ Jesus." Philippians 4:6-7

Misunderstandings

"Mama," I said as I sat down to eat lunch, "do you remember the time recently when we got in a scrape over how to take a cake out of the pan?"

"Kind of..." Mama said, thinking back. "Why do you ask?"

"I was thinking about that today. What I remember is that I was taking the cakes out of their pans and you came up and asked me to do it another way, but I didn't know why one way was better than another."

"Yeah, following instructions..." Mama mused.

"Well..." I responded, "I remember standing back and letting you do it and then doing it your way afterward. I was wondering why your way was better than mine. I think it was the way I asked the questions that made you upset."

"That may have been the case. It was a while ago, though."

"Yeah, it was a while ago." I responded. "The thing I remember best was how I felt and what I did afterwards."

"How was that?" Mama asked.

"Well, I remembered feeling so defeated and discouraged about our relationship that I went to my room and prayed, crying afterwards. I felt like I had tried everything with our relationship, and it wasn't improving. I cried out to God about it and asked Him to help me understand you and help you to understand me. I wanted to know how to make you feel honored and respected, but I was running out of strength. I think it's gotten much better now, though."

"Yes, I agree. It has gotten much better," Mama said. Mama and I have struggled with misunderstanding each other since I was very young.

Then, we talked about misunderstandings and how, in our flesh, the first thing we want to do is blame the other person for not understanding what we mean. This causes pain for the other person. Another way our flesh likes to respond is in self-pity, wallowing in the fact that we're misunderstood and allowing that to alter our countenance and make us look like we live in a world of despondency.

On the brighter side, have you ever thought about how misunderstandings can be a good thing? Misunderstandings are an opportunity for us to prove our love for others. When we truly endeavor to understand others, especially in hard times, it will be proof to them that we love and care. It's not easy, but was love really ever *meant* to be easy? Sharing love with others is a blessing, but it still requires work. When we fervently try to understand others, it will be *proof* to them that we love and care. Persevering though hard times will strengthen our commitment to the relationship. Our perseverance will also help those we struggle with feel special. So, learn to prove your love for your family by striving to understand them when they misunderstand you!

Misunderstandings are an opportunity for us to prove our love for others.

How Little Things Get Big and How to Keep Them Small

Little things like negative thoughts, misunderstandings, and blind spots can become huge problems in our lives if they are not dealt with properly. Remember, our thoughts will become words, and then actions, and eventually habits. We don't want to deal with bad habits, do we?

Misunderstandings can do just as much harm as negative thoughts. If we don't try to understand our parents, we allow the enemy to take his shovel and dig a huge pit between us and our parents. Then, we'll have to work (and work hard!) to fill it back up with good things. As we discussed earlier, blind spots need attention, but you may not even know they are there. That's where humility steps in. It's so important to listen to what others have to say about how you can grow. Humility is key for success in every area of life.

A *humble person* serves.

A *humble person* loves the unlovable.

A *humble person* presses on and tries to understand the non-understandable.

A *humble person* gives and gives and gives because they know how much Christ gave for them.

A *humble person* thinks better of others than of themselves.

A *humble person* listens to advice and applies it to life.

A *humble person* perseveres and rejoices in the Lord.

A *humble person* doesn't fear, but instead trusts God's plans.

"Therefore humble yourselves under the mighty hand of God, that He may exalt you in due time, casting all your care upon Him, for He cares for you." 1 Peter 5:6-7

5 Ways to Ruin Your Relationship with Your Parents

"I have set before you life and death, blessing and cursing; therefore choose life, that both you and your descendants may live." Deuteronomy 30:19b

There are plenty of very effective ways to tear apart the relationship you have with your parents. Sometimes the things that wreak havoc on our relationships with our parents are hidden sins. Other times, they are sins we know about and either don't want to change or don't know how to change. To my relief, you are probably not reading this book so you can learn how to make your relationships worse. I trust you'll take this chapter with a grain of salt and *learn how to avoid* pride, discontentment, bitterness, dishonesty, and dishonor!

1) Pride

> "By pride comes nothing but strife, but with the well-advised is wisdom." Proverbs 13:10

Pride is a big one. That's why it's put first in this chapter. According to the above verse, it's probably safe to say most arguments can be traced back to pride. When we have pride in our hearts, it will come out in our interactions with our parents. We have to watch out, because pride often sneaks in without being seen. I love the way a friend of mine put this: "Usually, we don't just wake up one morning, march up to our parents, and say, 'I think I know more than you do!' Pride comes out in our day-to-day interactions and will get bigger if we don't nip it in the bud."

Here's an example: One day, Sam was cleaning his room, and his mom came by to point out some things he left out. Sam replied, "They're ok there, Mom. I don't want to put them away."

Is that the right response? No. Sam should have either picked them up or asked his mom respectfully if it was ok to keep the items there. Did you catch the pride in Sam's attitude?

Sam responded as if he knew more than his mom did by telling his mom it was fine to have his stuff there. He should have either put the things away immediately or *asked* his mom if it would be ok for him to leave the things there and then *respectfully* given her the reason he wanted to keep them there. Keep in mind that sometimes we don't see when we're being disrespectful. If our parents tell us we are being disrespectful, chances are that they're right. At least we may have made them feel disrespected. We don't want them to feel that way, do we?

I know plenty of adult-aged children who are more experienced or more knowledgeable in *certain things* than their parents are, but that is no reason for them to boast or act better or smarter. Do we really prefer looking good to pursuing a healthy relationship? So often, that's exactly what we do (without realizing it, of course). But, we still to it, and it's pride - a sin for which Jesus died.

"Your parents' position needs to be respected more than their intelligence."

-My mom

"Let nothing be done through selfish ambition or conceit, but in lowliness of mind let each esteem others better than himself." Philippians 2:3

"Thus says the Lord: 'Let not the wise man glory in his wisdom, let not the mighty man glory in his might, nor let the rich man glory in his riches; but let him who glories glory in this, that he understands and knows Me, that I am the Lord, exercising lovingkindness, judgment, and righteousness in the earth. For in these I delight,' says the Lord." Jeremiah 9:23-24

2) Discontentment

What would your response be if you went to a friend's birthday party and gave him or her a nice, expensive gift (paid for with your own money), and your friend just gave it a quick glance and put it aside without saying anything? Would you feel appreciated as a friend or would you feel rejected and sad?

When we were little, we didn't know how to say "please" or "thank you," but our parents loved us anyway. Sometimes, we threw big, ugly fits, but our parents still took care of us. We may have even told them how selfish they were for not doing what *we wanted* them to do in the way *we wanted* it done, but they still provided our food, clothing, and shelter. Plus, they loved us and wanted to do nice things for us! There is so much to be grateful for about our parents.

Proverbs 30:15 says that the leech has two daughters that cry "give, give!" That's because leeches are little worms that just take and take. They cling to skin and suck blood, leaving tiny, itchy welts. All they want in relationships is what they can get, and they don't think of what they can give in return.

Do we want to act like a leech, sucking energy and time from family and friends without giving in return? Unfortunately, it's far too easy to act like a leech. Have you ever been given one nice thing, then another, asked your parents for something else, and then complained of hunger? If it wasn't recently, maybe it was a few years ago. I know I've done this. Have you?

We should appreciate and enjoy everything our parents do for us. Saying "thank you," and really meaning it, will help bind you together with your parents. Also, joyfully helping them with what they need to get done or doing something that would bless the family will help them feel appreciated for who they are and what they do for you.

3) Bitterness

Oftentimes, when children get hurt by their parents, they allow bitter feelings and grudges to penetrate their thoughts. When we're being instructed or punished, it's easy to believe the lie that our parents really don't love us. We're tempted to think that they ask us to do difficult things because they don't like us. We need to be sure not to think this way, because it is the beginning of a negative thought catastrophe!

I do not know of any parents whose purpose in life is to hurt their children. Seriously, do parents get together with friends so they can talk about how to hurt their children and make their lives miserable? Your mom and dad love you! They want the best for you. However, it's almost a given that at some point in your life, you will actually be unintendedly hurt by your parents. So, what should you do when that happens?

The first and most natural human response is to shift blame and harbor feelings of pain and bitterness, but those responses lead down a cheerless road. Eventually, those choices can cut off a relationship with parents entirely, so be

"And forgive us our debts as we forgive our debtors."
Matthew 6:12

careful! A bitter response will lead to more pain down the road than the offense initially inflicted.

The other option is forgiveness, which is a more difficult mountain to climb at first, but in the long run, it is much better than a ruined relationship.

Forgiveness is "clearing the record of those who have wronged me and allowing God to love them through me."[1] *"Clearing the record"* means erasing all previous wrongs and not bringing them back to mind again. *"Allowing God to love them through me"* means to do for others what Jesus has done for us. This is to show unconditional love and care, even to those who have hurt us tremendously. This road requires *lots* of humility. It's difficult to be humble...terribly difficult. That's why forgiveness is more of an upward climb. Humility takes courage. Forgiveness is a place where humility and courage meet so that a relationship can be restored and strengthened. That's the place we want to go.

Humility is Courageous

---

[1] Institute of Basic Life Principles "Operational Definition of Character Qualities"

4) Dishonesty

There are many ways to be dishonest, so let's get started recognizing those ways now so we can leave them in the dust! Dishonesty is the result of seeking a reward for ourselves in living life our way, rather than seeking the blessings of God in His way and timing. Three verses from Proverbs especially stand out to me about dishonesty:

> *"The truthful lip shall be established forever, but a lying tongue is but for a moment." Proverbs 12:19*

> *"Lying lips are an abomination to the Lord, but those who deal truthfully are His delight." Proverbs 12:22*

> *"A righteous man hates lying, but a wicked man is loathsome and comes to shame." Proverbs 13:5*

After reading those verses, can you think of any good reason to cover up sin or even tell a teeny, tiny, white lie? It looks to me like liars get exposed and are not successful. God is disgusted with lies. Liars aren't fun to be around. Liars also bring shame on themselves. Is there anything that interests you about lying here? Not me!

Dishonesty can sneak into our lives in subtle ways. For example, it is possible to be *deceitful* without actually telling any "lies." As long as no one asks, no one knows, and no one lies. Right? *Well*, if you know it's wrong, and you are hiding it, it's <u>deceit</u>. By hiding things in your life, you may be misleading others to think you are someone you really are not.

You can be deceitful for only a little while - be sure your sin will find you out! Luke 12:2 says, "For there is nothing covered that will not be revealed, nor hidden that will not be known."

When I was in middle school, I lied to my parents about doing my schoolwork. For a while, I got away with lying, but when my parents found out, I had to redo some work. All this redoing of work panned out to be more laborious and painful for me than if I had just done my homework in the first place. While I was still hiding my little secret, I could not be as free to be around them because I was afraid I would get found out. After I was found out, they could no longer trust what I said. Also, my lying made my parents sad and injured their trust in me. So, instead of being closer to them, my sin separated me from them. Only when trust had been rebuilt could I have a good relationship with them again.

Deceit is a huge temptation for many people, not only in the area of schoolwork, but also in chores and other things that *seem* to be convenient or fun to hide for a while. It is so important to learn <u>now</u>, while we are young, to be 100% honest in everything. We must be ever-vigilant to make sure we're walking in the light of God's truth.

Do you know that we often lie because we are afraid? We fear the consequences of people finding out who we really are. We lie to protect the way people view us. But, lying will only make us look worse in the long run. In addition, lying will also make it harder to make up for our wrongs.

Lying is the opposite of faith and trust in God's love for us. Faith trains our hearts to say and do what is harder and less convenient in the moment, with hope that God has better things in store for our future. Faith enables us to obey God with joy, even though we can't see the outcome of our actions.

Without faith, we can't please God (Heb. 11:6). Instead of seeing how close we can get to the edge of sin and lying, we need to do the opposite and lean on Jesus more and more through faith. The closer we grow to Jesus, the harder it will be to fall over the cliff of sin. Spend time with Him and learn to be grieved by any hint of sin in your life. Jesus was mocked, broken, bruised, and died in agony over these very sins we have committed! Hate sin because it hurts Jesus. It's impossible to have sweet fellowship with our Lord while we're hiding sin!

Conscience: That little voice inside you that keeps getting in the way.

-Treasures in the Snow

> "Behold, the Lord's hand is not shortened, that it cannot save; nor His ear heavy, that it cannot hear. But your iniquities have separated you from your God; and your sins have hidden His face from you, so that He will not hear." Isaiah 59:1-2

5) Dishonor

There are two kinds of dishonor: open, purposeful dishonor and accidental dishonor. Open dishonor begins in the mind and heart and then leads to doing and saying things that bring pain and hurt to our parents. Accidental dishonor happens when we cause our parents pain without knowing it.

Any of the four points previously discussed (pride, discontentment, bitterness, and dishonesty) are ways to dishonor our parents. Anything that hurts your relationship with your parents instead of building it up dishonors them. Dishonoring your parents also dishonors God, since He asked us to honor our parents in the first place. We will talk more about how to honor parents later, but for now, we will dive into understanding how to avoid dishonor.

Not Listening

If you're looking for a good way to make your mom or dad have a bad day, don't listen to them. Of course, none of you would do that. So, ahem, if you're looking for ways to help your parents have a *great* day, listen to them! Listen to their stories, accept their instruction, laugh with them, and enjoy their company.

It's not always easy for me to listen to my parents, especially if I think I've heard the same thing for the ten trillionth time. It's so tempting to think, "Ugh! Why are they saying that again?" However, I must understand that God has a purpose for everything.

"And we know that all things work together for good to those who love God, to those who are the called according to His purpose." Romans 8:28

Instead of enduring our parents' instruction in gloomy silence, perhaps if we purposed to listen to them and interacted in a positive way about what they have said, then they would not feel like they need to tell us the same things over and over again. One way to interact positively is reflection. If your mom has asked you to do something, the reflective thing to do would be to either repeat back to her what she said, or ask for clarifications as needed. This would help her have confidence that you heard what she said and are planning to do it.

Hearing instructions numerous times can be annoying. Can we *learn* anything from repetitive instruction? We can rejoice that we get to grow in humility and longsuffering, knowing that every trial God sends has a purpose and can strengthen our faith (Jas. 1:2-4). We can also be ready to show our parents love by listening to them, knowing that they have shown us love many times when we didn't even deserve it. Our parents are a blessing, and their instruction will make us wise, *given* we listen to it.

> "Listen to counsel and receive instruction, that you may be wise in your latter days." Proverbs 19:20

> "A fool despises his father's instruction, but he who receives correction is prudent." Proverbs 15:5

Half-Way There

Sometimes, in our minds, we think we're listening to our parents, but our body language communicates differently. I call this "partial honor." It's not really honor. It's *kind of* doing what you're supposed to, but it's only half-way there. Which one of these children really honored their parents by listening *all the way*?

a. John sat on his bed looking at a book while his mother gave him instructions for mowing the lawn. After she was finished, he nodded his head and mumbled a reluctant, "Ok."

b. Holly read her list for the day and

then slouched on the couch in a pout. After her mom asked her to go do her list, she stomped off to complete it.

c. Andy was playing with his trucks when mother walked into the room with a request for Andy to change over the laundry. Andy looked up, stopped playing with his trucks, made eye contact with his mom, and said with a smile, "I'd be glad to!" Then, he hurried off to complete the job.

d. Janice was about to take her puppy on a walk when her mother came over and talked to her about how to study better for school. Meanwhile, Janice petted and talked sweetly to her puppy, only pausing periodically to pay attention to her mom.

What do you think? Andy had the best response, didn't he? He didn't just say "ok" or passively listen, he stopped what he was doing to pay attention to his mom, responded to her respectfully, and then allowed her to see that he was making steps in the right direction. It's important that our parents know for sure that we're actually going in the direction of obedience, or they might feel like they have to repeat the same thing over again or raise their voice before we will choose to obey.

Sometimes, it's not possible to do what our parents want us to do right away. If we have a good reason to postpone an action, we could always respectfully ask, "Would it be ok if I clean my room *after* I finish reading this page of my book/eating my dinner/etc.?" By asking them for permission to postpone a task, they can know we're planning on following through with it.

The Eye that Mocks...

"The eye that mocks his father, and scorns obedience to his mother, the ravens of the valley will pick it out, and the young eagles will eat it." Proverbs 30:17

What is mocking? Mocking a parent is basically treating their advice as if it has no meaning or application to life. Mocking could be rolling eyes, shrugging shoulders, laughing about their advice, etc.

Think about this verse: "Rebuke is more effective for a wise man than a hundred blows on a fool" (Prov. 17:10). Imagine that there are two boys, both about the same age, both having the same bad day, and both with the same bad attitude. For the wise boy, it only takes one rebuke before he is sorry for what he has done. The foolish boy is given many rebukes and disciplines, but he still replies in disdain, "I don't get it!" and keeps doing the wrong thing. As a result, his authorities have to keep disciplining him. Which child do you want to be like? I'm thinking you've probably chosen to be like the wise son - it sounds a lot less painful!

It is foolish to mock, because in mocking, we show that we don't want to listen to wisdom. As a result, we are unable to grow in the ways in which our parents and authorities direct us. Proverbs 14:6 tells us that even though a mocker seeks wisdom, he doesn't find it. Wouldn't it be discouraging to seek and seek and seek, and not find anything at all? That's what Proverbs 14:6 is talking about. So, don't be a mocker, but instead, embrace rebukes and listen to instruction!

Rebellion

> "For rebellion is as the sin of witchcraft, and stubbornness
> is as iniquity and idolatry..." 1 Samuel 15:23a

For years, our family raised goats. As I remember, our goats
needed help with character development from time to time. It
was hard to get them to obey and take their focus off
themselves! One day, tugging at Chestnut's leash, I coaxed,
yanked, and pulled, yet nothing seemed to distract him from
his single-minded focus – the food our nanny goat was
currently enjoying.

Our human tendency toward rebellion can be paralleled to
the rebellion we saw in our goats. Goats are *very* sweet, trust
me, but when it comes to staying in the fence or obeying in the
midst of temptation (also known as "food distractions," in goat
vocabulary), many of them fall short, as we all do before God
(Rom. 3:23).

Goats love to eat. Even though goats can be trained on a
leash like a dog and have dog-like personalities, they have a
wandering eye for food. It may be grass, flowers, shrubs, or
trees. They really don't care. If the shrub looks good, they're
making a beeline to the nearest green leaf. As goat keepers, my
family and I had to be careful they didn't eat things that were
bad for them. Cherry trees and rhododendron bushes were
among the poisonous plants on our property that we had to
make sure they steered clear of. Unfortunately, the goats didn't
always understand that we had their best interest in mind.
They probably rebelled inwardly, thinking, "Hey, that looked
good! I could have eaten that! Why do you always yank me
away from every tasty-looking shrub? Ugggg!"

Every one of us has rebellion issues and desires to eat "poisonous food" of sorts. If we knew ahead of time the undesirable consequences of sin, we might not be so prone to rebel. In the same way, if our goats knew what it felt like to die of food poisoning, I'm sure it would have been much easier to keep them away from those poisonous plants! God doesn't want us to have to experience sin and its consequences before we decide to obey Him. He wants us to desire to do His will, listen to Him, and obey those He has set over us.

"I will instruct you and teach you in the way you should go; I will guide you with My eye. <u>Do not be like</u> the horse or like the mule, *which have no understanding*, which must be harnessed with bit and bridle, *else they will not come near you.* Many sorrows shall be to the wicked; but he who trusts in the Lord, mercy shall surround him." Psalm 32:8-10

Reflection:

1) Write down 3 ways your parents may feel dishonored by your actions or attitudes.

2) Record 3 ways you could show your parents more honor.

3) Ask your parents if there are any ways they think you could honor them better.

The Heart – Jesus' Home

"Keep your heart with all diligence, for out of it spring the issues of life." Proverbs 4:23

The heart is the beating pulse behind any relationship. It's a very important place. In the heart, we experience the love, joy, and peace of God through His Spirit. However, sometimes we become careless with our hearts and allow a distance to develop between ourselves and the Lord. Sometimes when our enemy, Satan, tells us lies, we believe them. When we believe Satan's lies, this impacts our attitudes, decisions, and ultimately confuses us. How can we live our lives so that our hearts are a place where Jesus desires to dwell? We must be purposeful to live for Christ every day, or else sin will creep in without us even realizing it.

The Man in White

The man your friends have told you so much about has just arrived. He now lifts his fist to knock on your front door. You open the door and are met by a man clothed in sparkling white. As you introduce him to your family, he doesn't hesitate to use his charms on everyone. He brought a gift for each family member, and insisted that each be kept and used.

At first, when you saw the gifts, you felt a little on edge. These were appealing gifts, but you would never have asked for them. In some cases, you would have even tried to graciously turn them down. But, they were *really nice*. They couldn't be all that bad. Or could they? The movies, pictures, video games, and magazines he gave seemed dark. The thing that made you decide to keep the magazine he gave to you was his winning smile, assurance that you'd enjoy it, and his personality, which made you feel almost as happy as he seemed, yet uneasy at the same time.

Nevertheless, you had heard so many good things about him from your friends that your family generously gave him a room down the hall. He stayed, almost too willingly. He helped your brother with his schoolwork, and even gave mom a hand in the kitchen. He kept giving gifts, too.

After reading the magazine he gave you, many new thoughts roamed your mind and a new freedom reigned with intensity. You started to become a different person, and your family changed, too. Perhaps they had been influenced by their gifts as well. At first, the change was nice, but over time, you didn't want to talk about these changes because they hurt. Mom and Dad had been arguing a lot, and Dad decided to leave for a while. You think it's because of a disagreement they had over an issue at home. While that's going on, you and your siblings seem to disagree on almost a daily basis. All you want to do is resort to your room, close the door, and comfort yourself with one of your visitor's gifts.

He's the only one in the house who seems to be ok with life. He's the only one who acts like life is going the way he wants it to - as if things are going as planned. He is the only one from whom you take any advice.

One day, your eyes caught a glimpse of another, darker fabric underneath the white clothes the visitor normally wore. You noticed it was stained with blood, and shivers went down your spine as his whole ugly, depraved, evil self was revealed in a most disturbing way. You said nothing. He quickly exited the room, leaving you feeling chilled, restless, and terrified. Your realization revealed a man clothed in black, ruthless, hatred and wickedness.

What had he been doing to your family all this time he'd been in your house? Where did he come from? All the risky little toys he had given you were immediately viewed with disgust. How could you have played the fool so easily? You won't call the man in white your guest anymore. You'll call him "the strange intruder" instead, because you've realized that that's exactly what he was.

Now you're trapped. Not only is your whole family in shambles, but your whole inner belief system has turned upside down and inside out. The guest you embraced was a deceiver, clothed in white only to conceal the fact that he couldn't do away with his darkness. As you try to read the Bible now, God seems distant, and sin so easy to fall for...

"The thief does not come except to steal, and to kill, and to destroy. I have come that they may have life, and that they may have it more abundantly." John 10:10

Guard Your Heart

The heart holds the belief system of a person. Just as the family in our story should have been careful about what they allowed into their home, we should also be careful with what we allow to influence our hearts. What we believe dictates what we do.

When we allow thoughts to seed themselves in our hearts, we can be sure that they will be lived out somehow. "...for out of it [the heart] spring the issues of life" (Prov. 4:23). If we allow many good seeds to grow in our hearts, good will be able to bubble out of our lives to bless others. The Bible explains that we can know something about who a person is on the inside by observing their day-to-day lives. Jesus used a parable to explain this. A tree is known by what type of fruit it produces. A bad tree will bear bad fruit and a good tree will bear good fruit (Mat. 12:33).

What we believe dictates what we do.

So how can we bear good fruit? We need to make sure we are good trees. Our roots should sink deep into God's Word; our leaves should enjoy the sunlight of God's love; and our branches should reach upward in praise to the Almighty. We also need to have a good system to filter out the world's polluting influences.

Ephesians 6:10-18 focuses on how we can protect ourselves from polluting influences by wearing God's spiritual armor. In order to prevent the arrows of lies and temptation from destroying our good efforts, we need a shield. We need a tall, strong, well-made shield to protect us! "Above all, taking the shield of faith with which you will be able to quench all the fiery darts of the wicked one" (Eph. 6:16).

We need to stand strong with faith in God whenever a dart comes flying our way. A practical way to do this is to keep "shield verses." For example, if you struggle with fear, you can quote 2 Timothy 1:7, "For God has not given us a spirit of fear, but of power and of love and of a sound mind." God has given us many other verses throughout His Word to use whenever we are facing trials. It is wise to meditate on God's Word day and night. That is one way we can guard our hearts. As you can see, God's Word is an indispensable part of our battle plan. As the psalmist says:

"Your word I have hidden in my heart, that I might not sin against You." Psalm 119:11

When we feel that Satan is trying to tempt us, we need to take up the shield of faith and the sword of the Spirit by trusting who God is for our needs and using His Word to protect us in the fight. Satan wants to affect our lives, but he usually begins by first affecting our thoughts. If we allow Satan's lies to affect our minds, Satan can come in and take over pieces of our heart, building "castles" on our heart's soil. Any piece of ground not founded in faith and surrendered to Christ gives easy access to the devil's destruction. He seeks to kill and to destroy, but Christ has come that we may live life more abundantly (Jn. 10:10).

Have you ever played a game of *Risk*? On the *Risk* playing board, there is a map of the world and a lot of little soldiers, cavalry, and cannons. The player's goal is to plant their military in as many countries as possible so they can take over the world. Our enemy would gladly take over our "world." In fact, both God and Satan would like to establish their power in various parts of our lives. The difference between the two is that one army desires to harm, and the other desires to bless. Both want to have control, but which will? That decision is up to you.

Much unlike a game of *Risk*, this spiritual battle we fight depends on *actual life choices*. God never forces His help on us. If God is going to have control in our lives, we have to allow Him to. A mentor of mine wisely told me, "God is a gentleman. He wants to help us, but He won't force His help on us. He wants us to allow Him to help us." God didn't make us robots to do whatever He programmed us to do. He wants a relationship with us. Unfortunately, since we are inherently sinful (Rom. 7:5), we naturally give place for the devil in our lives. So, we need to be super cautious to *keep* letting God have control! Meeting with God daily is so important because we need to constantly surrender our lives to Him and ask for His wisdom on how to live every day.

> "God is a gentleman. He wants to help us, but He won't *force* His help on us. He wants us to allow Him to help us." —Becky Keilen

God will seem distant to us when our hearts are being ruled by our own desires. When we obey God, however, He can bless us (Duet. 11:26-27). The center of God's will is always the best and safest place to be.

Tricky!

Recently, there was a season in my life where things were going very well for me. I felt so blessed. In the midst of all this blessing, I started to become carefree about the fact that I had an enemy. I couldn't see him working any harm. So, without thinking, I assumed a careless attitude. The Lord was merciful to point out this lack of vigilance on my part. He showed me how I need to stay strong, even when I don't see a need for it, and how I should always press on to know more about Him. Even when Christ seems comfortably near, I should *never* stop desiring more of Him. If I seem to be full, I should remember that He desires that my cup *overflow* with His love and power in my life (Ps. 23:5).

One day during this season of life, I was talking to my friend's dad on the phone, and out of the blue right before he hung up with me, he made an off-the-wall comment, "Patience, don't forget to put on your armor every day."

"That was interesting..." I thought.

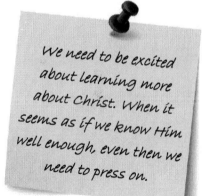

We need to be excited about learning more about Christ. When it seems as if we know Him well enough, even then we need to press on.

A few days later, I had a spiritual test. I was sitting at my desk mulling through the things I needed to do when all the sudden, I felt tired, lazy, and even grumpy. My list wasn't even exceptionally overwhelming, but slowly I slumped back in my chair and allowed my face to turn upside down and this strange mood to rule my heart.

Then, with alarm, I remembered that I'd felt this way before. "Oh great!" I thought, sarcastically. "This isn't good." So, I picked up some Bible memory work and went outside to memorize Scripture. About fifteen minutes later, to my surprise, I no longer felt lazy, grumpy, or tired.

Later, I went back to my friend's dad and asked him if he remembered what he had told me earlier on the phone. I was able to share with him how it had prompted me to think. We ended up having a discussion about how the spiritual battle is always being fought (no matter what!) and how it's always dangerous to mosey around without being *attentive* to the fight at hand.

The danger of living at ease is that we tend to forget to invest in our relationship with Jesus. Isn't it sad how we humans tend to talk to God more when we have troubles than when life is going well for us? Shouldn't we be at least thanking God when things are going well? Poor God. We misuse His mercy often! Jesus is never less deserving of our devotion at one time than another, and our enemy would always love to find someone he can destroy (1 Pet. 5:8). There is never any excuse for us not to seek the Lord!

Where We Set our Gaze

As we resist Satan's influences, we reject thoughts and lies that are meant to destroy us, such as "I am stupid," "Nobody likes me," "It is better for me to take this into my own hands than talk to God about it," as well as other negative thought processes that will be addressed in the following chapter. Too often, instead of focusing on Jesus and His strength to conquer these intruding thoughts, we get caught up in the lies and ideas, allowing Satan to steal our focus. We have a Commander who goes before us in battle, and if we, as soldiers, do not continue looking to Him, we will not know what we are supposed to be doing! The more we focus on the enemy's lies and fear his skill, the harder it will be to obey our commander, Jesus. When we focus on the foe, the going gets slow!

Sometimes people become afraid of our enemy, the devil's, schemes. However, this gives him even more strength in their lives! If we were to physically turn around and face the enemy, which we technically do when we fear him and think about him often, we set the front of our vulnerable bodies right across from where his arrows are pointed! We are protected in Christ if we follow wherever He leads, but if we start allowing the enemy to have our undue attention, we will stumble. When we focus on Jesus, He can keep us safe and we can find shelter in Him (Ps. 91:1-7). It makes so much sense that Jesus has asked us to fix our gaze upon Him alone!

When we focus on the foe, the going gets slow.

"...let us lay aside every weight, and the sin which so easily ensnares us, and let us run with endurance the race that is set before us, **looking unto Jesus,** the author and finisher of our faith." Hebrews 12:1-2

Even though we should not be overcome by fear of our enemy, at the same time, we cannot forget that we have one. 1 Peter 5:8 exhorts, "Be sober, be vigilant; because your adversary the devil walks about *like a roaring lion*, <u>seeking whom he may devour</u>." Then in the next verse, it goes on to say, "Resist him, steadfast in the faith, knowing that the same sufferings are experienced by your brotherhood in the world" (1 Pet. 5:9).

If you were in the middle of the jungle all by yourself and suddenly a lion pounced out in front of you with a mighty "ROAR!!," what would you do? Would you think, "Oh wow, it's a lion!? I've never seen one of those before. What an experience!! Look at those amazing teeth and its gorgeous mane! Oh, it looks interested in me. What a coincidence. I'm interested in it too! I think I want to pet it!"

Oh my...don't! You should definitely get away from there as quickly as possible! If the Bible describes the devil as a roaring lion, shouldn't we treat him the same way we would treat a hungry lion in real life? We never play with lions, we run from them! Don't play with sin; look to Jesus, and stay away!

Not Against Flesh and Blood

"For we do not wrestle against flesh and blood, but against principalities, against powers, against the rulers of the darkness of this age, against spiritual hosts of wickedness in the heavenly places. Therefore, take up the whole armor of God..." Ephesians 6:12-13a

When we see arguments and strife rising up in the family, we need to keep in mind that there is a battle being fought, not only between our family members, but much more importantly, in the spiritual realm! Ultimately, when we have problems, "...we do not wrestle against flesh and blood." We are fighting a spiritual battle (Eph. 6:12). You shouldn't fight against your parents, even though it can be tough to have a good relationship with them. In the times when you are tempted to argue with your parents, it's a good idea to fall on your knees and fight the battle in prayer.

Kim struggled with her parents on an almost daily basis. She grew up in a rigid home with a rough father who seemed to care more for himself than for others. Yelling was a common occurrence, and her mother was often the brunt of it. Kim started holding grudges against her father for his harsh and unloving treatment of herself and her mother. It wasn't long before those grudges turned into resentment. Kim also struggled relentlessly with her father's comparison between her and her siblings. She felt she could do nothing right and received much negativity. When Kim and her father argued, it would escalate and never get resolved. She simply gave into the bitterness and her resentment grew larger by the day. Unfortunately, Kim did not know to pray and take her burdens to her Heavenly Father. Instead, she felt trapped right where the enemy wanted her...hopeless.

Since the beginning of time, Satan has been up in arms against anything God sets in place. The father-child relationship can remind us of the relationship we have with our loving Heavenly Father. The respect we should give our parents can prepare us for a life-long journey of submitting to and obeying God. Satan would love to destroy each of these precious relationships and more! We need to guard our hearts and not allow the enemy to have the slightest ground in our lives.

God would love to give us the good things He has in store, but first, we need to seek Him. Those who seek find and those who knock will see opened doors (Mat. 7:7-8). Family relationships are *good things*. How can we seek first God's kingdom in our relationships with family members?

- Pray for them (Jas. 5:16)
- Serve them in love (Gal. 5:13)
- Support them with encouraging words (1 Thes. 5:11)
- Love them no matter what they do (1 Jn. 3:16)
- Love the Lord – He is our ultimate reward (Gen. 15:1)

"But seek the kingdom of God, and all these things shall be added to you. Do not fear, little flock, for it is your Father's good pleasure to give you the kingdom." Luke 12:31-32

Regaining Surrendered Ground

If our lives are like a battlefield and the enemy has worked his way in so that all that is left for God is one teeny weeny piece of land, what should we do? Is it hopeless? Is God strong enough to rescue our lives even after we've thrown it away to the enemy?

Our friend, Kim, from the previous page, allowed the enemy to build a stronghold of fear in her life. She was afraid of her father. She was often silent and nervous around him. As Kim grew in her walk with God, however, she realized that her problem was not so much found in her relationship with her dad as it was found in the spiritual war between God and Satan. The closer she got to God, the more her hope for the future grew. In order to grow in this way, she had to forgive her father. With God's help, she was able to view her situation from

God's point of view and see that her father didn't realize what he was doing to hurt his family. Her dad loved her, but had been hurt by his past and didn't know how to heal from it, so he resorted to anger. This realization of Kim's did not fix her father's anger problem, but it did free her from her bondage to her negative thoughts and fears. By obeying God, she allowed Jesus to retake the ground in her heart that she had unknowingly given to the enemy. God lifted her out.

"He also brought me up out of a horrible pit, out of the miry clay, and set my feet upon a rock, and established my steps. He has put a new song in my mouth – praise to our God; many will see it and fear, and will trust in the Lord."
Psalm 40:2-3

Obedience and Victory

It is so important to obey God. Many people cringe at the thought of "obedience," because freedom seems like so much more fun. However, a life lived in "freedom," as the world defines it, is actually slavery to sin. The world defines freedom as doing whatever we want whenever we want to do it. However, disobeying God is giving in to Satan, which leads to bondage. As Christians, we have been set free from sin. So, why live the life in which we were once mistreated slaves? Paul explains that the end of sin is death.

"Do you not know that to whom you present yourselves slaves to obey, you are that one's slaves whom you obey, whether of sin leading to death, or of obedience leading to righteousness?" Romans 6:16

One of the differences between being a slave of sin and being a slave of righteousness is the places they each lead to.

One has an end in shame and death, the other in honor, life, and joy. Which will you choose?

Set Your Gaze Ahead

Set your gaze ahead - on Heavenly things - where Christ is seated at the right hand of God (Col. 3:1). Wear your armor, because no matter how subtle the battle seems at the time, a fight is at hand (Eph. 6:18). Think on true and praiseworthy

things, not only because we need encouragement and refreshment, but also because thinking about right and good things will help us become better soldiers (see Phil. 4:8). Set your gaze on Christ, as Peter learned to do on the stormy sea. Sing praises to Christ even in the darkest of nights. Experience the truth, that as long as you have your gaze fixed on Jesus, you can and will stand firm!

"For the weapons of our warfare are not carnal but mighty in God for pulling down strongholds, casting down arguments and every high thing that exalts itself against the knowledge of God, *bringing every thought into captivity to the obedience of Christ.*" 2 Corinthians 10:4-5

Your Next Visitor

You suddenly hear another knock at your door and hurry to open it. With surprise, you see a visitor in white...again. But, you sensed a wonderful peace.

"I've been calling your name over and over, but you haven't heard me. I love you," He said.

Joy mingled with grief and pain were swallowed as you fell into His open arms. You were so ready to completely surrender your life to Him (Jas. 4:7). You knew exactly who He was. This was Jesus, who had paid for your salvation and who would free you from your past. You chose to make Him Lord, and to leave your old, sinful ways behind. It was finalized (Rom. 10:9, Lk. 13:5). You accepted His offer of freedom and salvation and became His child (Jn. 1:12).

You invited Him into your house and took Him to your room. Suddenly, you noticed a sad expression on His face and followed it to where He gazed. As He walked around the room and shifted His eyes from item to item, you realized these items were gifts your former guest, the "intruder," had given to you. You could almost see tears in His eyes. He picked one up and turned it over in His hand.

"Jesus, you can have that," you blurted emotionally. Instantaneously[2], it vanished. This one freeing experience led you to surrender item after item, circumstance after circumstance, and person after person to God's control[3]. And as you did so, you made room in your heart for your wonderful

---

[2] In real life, surrender is not usually instantaneous. It can be a long, hard process that involves surrendering and re-surrendering multiple times. Remember, Jesus said to take up your cross daily (Lk. 9:23).

[3] These may also be things that steal your joy and/or push God, your parents, your family members, or the local body of believers away.

new Savior and Master to take residence, to be King, and to reign.

Finally, He had the place of honor in your room, in your heart, and in your life. You reasoned that if He *was* Lord, then He should have the right to remove anything from your life He wanted to.

"Child..." He said, and you turned your head to see Him. "You have given me the place of honor in your life, and I will honor you for that (Jn. 12:26). But, you have an enemy to whom you have formally given place to in your life. He will seek to devour and destroy you. He is ruthlessly jealous for your life, not to save it, but to destroy it. Call to Me whenever he knocks at your door. I will be right here. Remember, I will do nothing unless you give me permission to. But, I *will* answer mightily when you call."

"Call to Me, and I will answer you, and show you great and mighty things, which you do not know." Jeremiah 33:3

"It shall come to pass that before they call, I will answer; and while they are still speaking, I will hear." Isaiah 65:24

Battlefield Tips

Most of the battle takes place in the mind and heart, so it's important to fill those places with God's truth! Here are some hints:

- *Pick a verse to think about each day.* Write it on a 3X5 card and carry it around so that you can pull it out to read as necessary. You could also write a verse on a sticky note and put it somewhere you can see it throughout the day. "For the word of God is living and powerful, and sharper than any two-edged sword..." Hebrews 4:12

- *Replace worldly music with uplifting music with a Christ-centered message.* What is your music like? Does it encourage you to live for God? Does is lead your spirit into worship, or does it encourage you to think or act selfishly? "Let the words of my mouth and the meditation of my heart be acceptable in Your sight, O Lord, my strength and my Redeemer." Psalm 19:14

> "We don't have a choice. We are in a spiritual battle whether we like it or not."
> —My dad

- *Watch your influences.* Are the characters you watch on the television good or bad influences in your life? Do they honor their parents? Could you be picking up bad habits or attitudes from them?

- *Choose friends wisely.* Scripture infers that we will become like those we are around. We want to find wise friends so that we can become wise with them (See Prov. 13:20 and Prov. 12:26).

- *Pray about everything you do and about every concern you have.* "Rejoice always, pray without ceasing, in everything give thanks; for this is the will of God in Christ Jesus for you" (1 Thess. 5:16-18). "Therefore humble yourselves under the mighty hand of God...casting all your care upon Him, for He cares for you" (1 Pet. 5:6-7).

- *Claim power over the enemy.* Because we are in Christ and Christ is in us, we have authority over evil in Jesus' name. Pray against evil and trust God for strength. "Be sober, be vigilant; because your adversary the devil walks about like a roaring lion, seeking whom he may devour. Resist him, steadfast in faith..." (1 Pet. 5:8-9a).

- *Find a prayer partner to support you in battle.* Wouldn't it be awful if every soldier had to slay his giants single-handedly? It may sound valiant, but in reality, it is actually more valiant, more challenging, more encouraging for the body of Christ, and better for you when you are transparent about your struggles with others. "Confess your trespasses to one another, and pray for one another, that you may be healed. The effective, fervent prayer of a righteous man avails much" (Jas 5:16).

- *Take every thought captive.* "...bringing every thought into captivity to the obedience of Christ" (2 Cor. 10:5).

- *Know that God wants to show you how strong He is, not how strong you can be.* Much of spiritual victory is actually surrender to Christ. "'Not by might nor by power, but by My Spirit' says the Lord of hosts" (Zech. 4:6b).

- *Remember that **the battle is the Lord's**!* "For the battle is the Lord's..." (1 Sam. 17:47b).

- *Praise the Lord that He has already won the war!* Although we still have small battles to fight, God has already won the war. Let's fight with Him! "Having disarmed principalities and powers, He made a public spectacle of them, *triumphing* over them in it" (Col. 2:15).

The heart is the seat of our belief system and the place from which our decisions stem. Therefore, it is crucial to guard it and make sure that God is in control. In the midst of the battle, we can rejoice, knowing that God will use tribulations for good to make our character more like Christ (Rom. 5:2-8). By His grace, we have the ability to choose to follow Christ and to put our hearts under His reign. Through His name, we have the all we need to persevere in making our hearts Christ's home.

14 Lies Children Believe About Family Relationships

"And you shall know the truth, and the truth shall make you free." John 8:32

How does the evil "man in white" affect our day-to-day lives? Is it not by making us believe untruths about God, ourselves, and others? Part of the secret of staying out of Satan's traps is recognizing what his traps are. This chapter contains come-backs to untruths people believe and ties them into family relationships. You may want to either read through the whole chapter, or look through it for lies you believe and simply read those sections.

When we realize we have believed something about God, ourselves, or others that is untrue, we have to develop a plan for how to dispose of it. Some of these "lies" I talk about in this chapter may not really be lies, but simply half-truths or negative thought processes. It would be believing a lie to think that holding on to those thoughts would be beneficial for you. One simple way to tell whether or not a certain thought process is beneficial and right is to compare it to the Word of God. If it is not in line with God's Word, it is not true. God wants us to know the truth:

> "And you shall know the truth, and the truth shall make you free." John 8:32

Sometimes it is hard to get out of the habit of believing a certain lie. In those cases, it is powerful to find a Scripture verse that relates and use it over and over again every time the lie comes up. Quote the verse. Pray the verse. Sing the verse. Simply find ways to remind yourself of the *truth*. For example, if you believe you are worthless to your family and all those around you, you could read the verse in Psalm 139 that says "I am fearfully and wonderfully made..." If God made you to be wonderful, then you must not be worthless. You now have an opportunity to embrace God's worth for your life by thinking about the truth every time you are tempted to believe that you are worthless. The same thing applies to all the lies addressed in this chapter. Here are some things to keep in mind as you read:

"...It's not enough to ask, 'Do I believe this lie?' Each of us must also ask, 'Do I *live* as though I believe this lie?'"
Nancy Demoss Wolgemuth

- Am I believing this lie?
- If I am believing this lie, how can I expose that area of my life to truth again?
- Has believing this lie damaged my relationship with the Lord? Do I need to apologize to God for disbelieving Him?
- Has believing this lie damaged any of my relationships with my family members? Do I need to apologize to them for anything hurtful I've said or told them because I believed this lie?

The Cycle of a Lie

A lie starts off as a thought or a feeling. We have a choice whether to reject or accept it. If it is accepted, a lie can become a real part of our lives. It's good to know that any believable lie has a lot of half-truths in it.

For example, two brothers, Dan and Kirk were playing together outside. Dan, the older brother, was jumping over lawn furniture. He did not realize that his little brother, Kirk, would want to do what he was doing. He also didn't realize that playing his "conquer the heights" game might injure his parent's lawn furniture.

When Dan's mom came outside, she was shocked by her mature son's ill-thought out activity. With fear and disappointment, she harshly reprimanded him, especially on being a bad example to his impressionable brother. Dan loved being a good example to his brother and was deeply hurt that his mother had told him that he was a bad example. After this situation, he believed he was not a good example. Dan's mother did not realize that she had hurt her son's feelings, but she did notice that for the next couple days, he was not acting like himself anymore. Now, she had more reasons to tell her son he was not being a good example. His diligence was slacking and his countenance was distant and prideful. She reinstated that he needed to improve. Later, his father told Dan that he was not up to par. Dan regressed even further. He had become what he wasn't originally because he believed the lie.

See how Dan cycled through from believing to becoming. How can he stop his behavior from getting even worse? By recognizing the lie, rejecting and fighting against it, and by seeking improvement instead. This is the same with many other lies that are discussed in this chapter.

{Lie Chapter Topic Index}

-Lies About God-

- God gave me the wrong parents. -123-
- When my parents mess up, God does, too. -124-

-Lies About My Parents-

- My parents don't understand me. -126-
- My parents don't appreciate my desires or goals. -128-
- My parents don't love me and don't have time for me. -131-
- My parents should be perfect. -132-
- My parents need to be the way I want them to be. -133-
- My parents' counsel is invalid because they don't follow it either. -135-

-Lies About Myself-

- My parents don't love me. -140-
- I don't make my parents happy. I can't do anything right. -141-
- Good relationships with my siblings are not important. -143-
- I'm too young to do anything for God. -145-
- I am not capable of what my siblings are capable of. I am less valuable than others around me. My family would be better without me. -146-
- Serving my family at home is not an eternal investment. -148-

Lies About God

God gave me the wrong parents.

If you believe this about your parents, consider *why* you think this way. Are you comparing your parents with your friend's parents? Do you think that if your parents acted differently you would have a better chance to grow?

Anything along this train of thought will only make you discontent. You have the parents you have, period. You can't change that. You can either love it or hate it. But, hating it will end in bitterness. Then you'll be both discontent and bitter! Doesn't sound like the way to a happy life, does it?

Also, when there are relational struggles, it's normally a two-sided ordeal. It takes two to argue. If you focus on how wrong your parents are or how discontent you are with them, you won't have any room in your heart to think of how *you* can grow and learn through the difficult situation or how *you* can make the situation better.

When our parents don't treat us the way we want them to, we can pray that God will help our responses to our parents to be loving and excellent in spirit. When I speak of being excellent in spirit, I mean having an attitude in which joy, humility, love, and honor are all wrapped together along with a craving desire to glorify the Lord. Sadly, the world is full of children who may not even think about honoring their parents. We need to shine as bright lights in the area of honor. Then, when others

watch us respond lovingly to our parents' instruction, they can observe and follow.

Toolkit

-*Lie: God gave me the wrong parents.*-
- 2 Corinthians 10:12
- Romans 8:28
- Jeremiah 29:11
- Psalm 139:13

When my parents mess up, God does, too.

God puts people over us to care for us. When the caretakers He sets over us make mistakes, God hasn't failed us. He can *still* be honored through our lives. We can thank Him for trials and mistakes because we know trials produce Christ-like character and draw us closer to Him (Rom. 5:3-5).

Have you ever seen the underside of a quilt while it's being made? It's full of loose pieces of string, ugly knots, and maybe even missing pieces here and there. It's not pretty. Similarly, what we see of our lives often look like the underside of a quilt. We can only see the struggles, difficulties, and failures. However, God is piecing our lives together in much the same way a quilter would piece together a quilt. The difference for us in this analogy is that God, the quilter, can see the top, nice-looking side, from heaven. He can understand why we may feel discouraged about His "progress," because all we can see from down here on Earth is the unfinished underside full of relational strain and imperfections. From time to time, in His mercy, God allows us to catch a glimpse of the masterpiece He's piecing together, which gives us renewed strength and hope to continue forward. Quilt-making is a long and tedious process, and so is working on your relationship with your parents. In the end, both the Heavenly Quilter and His piece of art, you, will be able to look back in gratitude for every loose end and fraying block, knowing that everything was ultimately worked out to bring Christ honor and glory through our relationships.

Even when we see a mountain of mistakes and imperfections, God can use them if we allow Him to. He can take a mess and make it a beautiful picture of grace that will shine forth His love to multitudes of others who need to know that God can, and does, use imperfect lives.

When our parents mess up, God is not messing up. Both we and our parents mess up often and through these failures, God can be proven strong (2 Cor. 12:9-11). In our weakness, He can work mightily. He can teach us as we go through our trials and can strengthen us to achieve victory in situations we may face in the future. Do not lose hope. Press onward in the strength of the Lord.

"He is the Rock, His work is perfect; For all His ways are justice, A God of truth and without injustice; Righteous and upright is He." Deuteronomy 32:4

Toolkit

-Lie: When my parents mess up, God does, too.-

- Philippians 1:6
- Deuteronomy 32:4
- Romans 5:3-5
- 2 Corinthians 12:9-11

Lies About My Parents

My parents don't understand me.

Every child will have a different home experience and, therefore, will appreciate different viewpoints for combatting the negative thought that their parents don't understand them. It is impossible for parents to perfectly understand their children at all times. I write with this in mind. However, when we believe that our parents don't understand us, we tend to clam up and stop pursuing a relationship with them because we simply assume, "Ah, they don't understand."

Personally, when I have felt that my parents don't understand me, my greatest weapon against negative thoughts has been praise. Praise turns negativity into joy, similarly to how hot water can turn the dry instant pudding powder we find in cardboard boxes into a delicious dessert. Find everything and anything positive about them, take the time to appreciate it. Let them know you appreciate it. In addition to praising my parents, I might also praise God for the opportunity I've found to grow in character through the trial of parents who don't seem to understand my point of view.

Another thing that helps is blessing them verbally. Anytime my parents do something that upsets me, I've noticed that getting upset back never helps. I like to turn my negative train of thought around and wonder, "What character qualities might they need that I can bless them with?" (I will bless them out loud in a place they cannot hear.) I let myself overflow with requests to God for their well-being. If there's anything that has bothered me, such as a lack of love, insensitivity, etc., I am sure to pray for that too. It is hard to remain upset at someone while genuinely and actively praying for their very best. I often follow this with asking God to forgive my selfish heart attitude, because if I was upset at them, chances are, nine out of ten times, I could have done something better, too.

An example of a blessing might go something like this: "Heavenly Father, please help my parent through this difficult day. Bless them with the grace to be kind and with the faith to trust you with anything they might be anxious about. Bless them with children who love and respect them. Bless them with abundant joy as they complete their tasks today and let this joy grow as the years continue on. Bless them with the ability to enjoy life to the fullest. Enable them to follow You completely in every area of their life. Be by their side and help them know that you are there for them and love them. Pour out blessings on them until they don't have room enough for more, Lord. In Jesus' name, Amen."

Praying like that helps me to think about their needs more than my needs during difficult situations. Even though I feel like they do not understand me, I might not understand them either and just need to work my hardest to keep their best interest at heart. It is therapeutic and humbling to consider ways *I* may lack understanding for my parents. Ultimately, our differences serve as tests through which I can prove my love for them.

Centering our focus on whether or not we are understood by others is not in harmony with God's way. The Bible tells us to seek first God's kingdom and His righteousness (Mat. 6:33). We want to be understood, of course, but we cannot pridefully and selfishly become grumps when people don't understand us. Our parents can't understand all of who we are, and we can't understand them completely either. However, we do know Who understands all. The prized dreams of our hearts are safe in the arms of the Almighty. He understands.

Toolkit

-Lie: My parents don't understand me-

- Hebrews 12:3
- Zephaniah 3:17
- Luke 6:31

My parents don't appreciate my desires or goals.

Sometimes we feel like our parents don't appreciate our goals. This feeling could surface for several reasons. Sometimes, we don't know when our "good ideas" are actually bad ones. Sometimes we may just be wanting to do something so badly that we pressure our parents and make them feel uninterested. At other times, our parents might think our ideas are good, but are meant for some other time.

If you feel like your parents don't appreciate your goals, first see if your goals align with God's. If they don't, you may need to re-order, re-think, postpone, or drop them. If your goals align with God's goals, you can respectfully explain them to your parents. If you sense tension, you can ask them if they would want you to do anything differently and, if so, why. This will not only help you avoid tension with them, but it will also help you to understand what *their goals* are for you, which is a very important part of understanding what they do as they train you.

In many cases, parents really want to show respect toward their children's desires, or at least want to listen to them talk about it. Sometimes, their busy schedules, frequent distractions, or lack of emotional energy can prevent them from showing the care and interest they really want their children to feel from them. In any case, it would be harmful for a child to become bitter over a parent's lack of care. It is important to keep the best in mind about both yourself and your parents. Sometimes a presumed "uncaring" parent may struggle themselves with feeling uncared for. They may have had a difficult upbringing or be going through a tough time. In these cases, we need to pray more for them and show them Christ's mercy.

Philippians 4:8 admonishes us to think about positive things, "...whatever things are *true*, whatever things are *noble*, whatever things are *just*, whatever things are *pure*, whatever things are *lovely*, whatever things are of *good report*, if there is *any virtue* and if there is *anything praiseworthy* – meditate on these things."

The thought that our parents don't care about our desires and goals is a negative thought. Negative thoughts put walls between relationships and make them more stressful. We should always try to think positively about our parents, surrender our thoughts to God, remember the good things our parents do for us, and believe the best of them in love. Find all good things about what they are communicating. Seek to appreciate their desires and goals.

> "... (love) bears all things, *believes all things*, hopes all things, endures all things. Love never fails."
> 1 Corinthians 13:7-8a

Toolkit

-Lie: My parents don't appreciate my desires or goals. -

- Philippians 4:8
- 1 Corinthians 13:7-8
- Proverbs 4:1
- Write 10 things you appreciate about your parents.

"There have been moments in life when Satan brought this lie to mind that no one understands me or appreciates me. My parents have taught me the principles of Scripture and how to combat Satan's lies with God's truth. When this lie comes, I immediately began to pinpoint in my mind every instance in the last several days, in which I can see someone demonstrating that they understood or loved me; every kind deed or word directed toward me. When I'm through with that, I can also list specific verses about or references to God's love toward me throughout my life. Sometimes I have praised myself, (not out loud to others but only in my head to myself), when I feel like I could use a compliment instead of a correction and no one else is offering any."

-Anna

My parents don't have time for me.

It may be true that your parents are in a serious time crunch and don't have much time at the moment. But, that doesn't mean they don't love you. Other times, it may be that you aren't seeing the opportunities to spend time with your parents. At times when you need a parent to be there for you and your parents aren't available, it's important to remember that God calls Himself our Heavenly Father (Lk. 11:11-13). Whenever we feel our earthly parents can't fill our needs, we should always run to our Heavenly Father. He wants us to rely on Him to supply all our needs. It is necessary to love and trust the parents that God has placed in our lives, but it is not healthy to rely on them to fulfill the needs that only our Heavenly Father can meet. Such needs include internal fulfillment, unconditional love, and steady hope.

Even though I have wonderful parents, I have *still* had times in my life where I have felt that they let me down. Oftentimes this "let down" was the result of high expectations that weren't fulfilled the way I wanted them to be fulfilled. God was a refuge in disappointments like these. He knows my needs and how to fulfill them much better than my earthly parents can.

How often do we look for fulfilment in people, things, and possessions and forget to find our joy in the Lord? Could we be looking for fulfillment in our poor, dear parents? Are we downtrodden when life messes up? We all need someone like God...but only God can be God. So, let's invite Him to be all He should be in our lives.

Jesus did not promise us an easy life, but He did promise us joy and abundant living (Jn. 15:11; Jn. 10:10). Being a Christian literally means living as Christ did. Did Christ live an easy life? (See Isaiah 53:3, Hebrews 12:3, and the Gospels for more on this). It only makes sense to assume that the One who made us and suffered for us would know best. Next time you feel like your parents don't love you or have time for you, pray for a positive relationship with your parents and seek the fulfillment that only our Heavenly Father can give.

Toolkit

-Lie: My parents have time for me. -

• Luke 11:9-13
• John 15:11

My parents should be perfect.

When God made man, everything was perfect. When Adam and Eve took that first juicy bite of the forbidden fruit, they realized they had done something awful. They frantically hid themselves, hoping no one would find them (See Genesis 3).

We are Adam and Eve's descendants. We are created just like them, except with an innate sin nature due to the fall. God made the world perfectly, and everything was wonderful until sin entered. Perhaps, sometimes, we feel like life *should* be as unspoiled as it was in the garden. You should be perfect; I should be perfect; they should be perfect; life should be perfect. But, it just doesn't happen that way.

You and I have parents who feel an urge to be perfect, too. Sometimes that's a lot for them to bear. Our perfectionistic attitudes won't help them any. We are here to obey, uplift, and *encourage* our parents. We are their children, their friends, their precious family members, and individuals they're pouring their hearts, time, and resources into. We are every bit as imperfect as they are, if not more so. So, let's pray for ourselves that God would save us from our selfish pride and give us humility and love for our parents that triumphs over the desire to see them as perfect. Yes, we can leave room for improvement, but still, love and graciousness should always abound over and beyond any remembrance of life's blemishes.

"As it is written: there is none righteous, no not one...for all have sinned and fall short of the glory of God." Romans 3:10,23

Toolkit
-Lie: My parents should be perfect. -

- Romans 3:10, 23
- James 4:10

My parents need to be the way I want them to be.

This is a lie that is easy to believe without even thinking about it. When there is a disagreement, it's always easier to blame the other person for causing the problem, for being stiff-necked, or perhaps for being just plain difficult. We think of different ways we wish they had responded and judge them for falling short. However, it is always humbler to look for ways *we* can change and work around life's little annoyances.

Proverbs 19:11 says "The *discretion* of a man makes him *slow to anger*, and his *glory* is to *overlook a transgression*." Strong's Concordances says the word "glory" literally means an ornament, a beautification, or even a sign of bravery.

Think about Jesus. Was He merciful or judgmental? How many sins have we committed (in our minds included) over the past two weeks? Would we like God to punish us for every single thing we did wrong? Because of Jesus' sacrifice on the cross, I have peace, forgiveness, and a High Priest who will bear my sins and help me in my weakness. Through His Word, He encourages me to forsake my sin and grow in righteousness. He is my best friend, even though I constantly prove how unworthy I am to be His child and a partaker of His grace. I am constantly reminded of areas in my life where I could grow or see improvement, but Jesus doesn't condemn me for not having those areas down pat and perfect (Rom. 8:1).

In this same way, Jesus wants us to take the grace He has given and share it with others (Col. 3:13). However, to love the way Jesus loves is a high calling. We need to continually rely on Christ's grace to strengthen us and ask for His love to flow through us into the lives of our parents and all those around us. This can be done as we continue in humility. The apostle Paul wrote, "let nothing be done through selfish ambition or conceit, but in lowliness of mind *let each esteem others better than himself*" (Phil. 2:3). Ask the Lord to help you imitate this humility Paul described. It might mean praising your parents for things they are doing well, or thanking them for advice they have given. In any case, this humility will be something you learn as you pray, ask questions of the Lord and others, and live it out daily.

"Judge not, that you be not judged. For with what judgment you judge, you will be judged; and with the measure you use, it will be measured back to you." Matthew 7:1-2

Toolkit

-Lie: My parents should be the way I want them to be. -

- Proverbs 12:15
- Proverbs 19:11
- Matthew 7:1-2

My parents' counsel is invalid because they don't follow it either.

Sometimes, when children see hypocrisy in their parents' lives, they feel justified in doing wrong things, too. It is natural and healthy to follow the examples of older people in our lives. However, we need to keep in mind that those examples are never perfect. Jesus is the only perfect example-setter we will ever have (Jn. 13:15).

We, as Christians, need to do our best to live righteously, whether our parents are doing the right things or not. We have no excuse. *God Himself* has died for us. Not only is it wrong to do wrong things, but it also hurts Jesus. Wouldn't it be painful for Christ to see us willfully live in sin after He has paid a great price to free us from it? Christ offers us so much. Why eat a dirt cookie when your favorite dessert is waiting on the table? And why continue in sin when He has sacrificed so much to free us from that very thing (Rom. 6:1-4)? Do you know that those who sin are slaves to what they do? As John 8:34 says, "Most

assuredly, I say to you, whoever commits sin is a slave of sin."
The following is an allegory depicting a slave in bondage to sin
and his ransom escape.

A Slave to Sin

Standing in the midst of a crowd of jeering scorners, an auction was
going on. I was on the platform, hands tied behind my back and body
bruised. I felt dejected and hopeless. My mind wandered back to the first
time I entered this awful life. I had a choice. I knew I did. I didn't have
to give in, but at the time it looked so appeasing, and it was fun at first. It
was great to be able to do things my own way. It felt good to rebel, be
crazy, and follow my friends. But, when I ran out of good fortune, my
friends left me with an old, oppressive ogre named Sin. I was trapped by
his schemes. Every time I tried to escape, I was only pulled deeper into
awful darkness by a burden that was too heavy to even think about. The
load seemed like an enormous black cloud hovering over my head. I
realized that I was trapped by Sin because I had allowed Sin to be my
master. I had fallen for it and played with that tricky, old liar. Finally, he
heartlessly sold me at auction...as a slave.

The auctioneer called out numbers, and a few people raised their
hands in agreement. As I looked around, there were only a few faces in
the crowd who didn't wear a grimace. Some looked depressed, others
angry, and still others hardened all over. One man in particular stood out
to me and made me shiver. His eyes were piercing, and his smile wicked.
He was dressed in black with a notable hat.

"To the gentleman in the black hat!" I heard the auctioneer shout.

I knew it! It was just my luck to go to the scariest looking one. He
was to be my new master. Somehow, I didn't even care where I went. I
felt so hopeless and heavy-hearted that my fondest dream was to simply

forget my troubles. I would go with that awful stranger knowing that life would be nothing but heartache and misery.

"Wait!" I heard someone yell from the back of the crowd. "I'll take the place of the slave myself. Let him go free!" The crowd suddenly, and unnaturally, hushed.

"What? What was he talking about?? Didn't he know how cruel slave owners could be?" I seriously didn't know what to think. I turned to look at the man in the black hat, and with one glare out of his squinted, narrow eyes, he grunted and motioned for his helpers to tie up the man who offered himself in my place.

The auctioneer cut my ropes saying, "You're free, and you'd better be happy...I've never seen anything like this before in my entire lifetime."

For the next few weeks, my mind was in a constant blur. Especially after I heard rumors of his mistreatment and death by that awful man. "Who would do give themselves willingly over to someone like that?" I wondered. "There is nothing he could gain from this sacrifice. Why did he do it? Why, why, why!?"

Something urged me to open my Bible, which was long buried away. I slowly pulled it out and dusted off its cover. As I opened it, the binding fell open to Romans, and I read:

"For when you were slaves of sin, you were free in regard to righteousness. What fruit did you have then in the things of which you are now ashamed? For the end of those things is death. But now having been set free from sin, and having become slaves of God, you have your fruit to holiness, and the end, everlasting life. For the wages of sin is

death, but the gift of God is eternal life in Christ Jesus our Lord."
Romans 6:20-23

Puzzled by these thoughts, I slept a wistful sleep. The following
morning, I woke and took a country road in the direction of the market.
Taken by surprise, I saw the mysterious man who saved me at the
auction. He turned to me, beaming with joy.

Without thinking, my thoughts spilled out, "Why? Why did you do
it? How could you think of becoming a slave for me? I thought you were
dead! How can you be here? Thank you. Thank you so much!"

"I did it because I love you. Have you not heard? I am not a slave to
sin, I conquered sin (Col. 2:15). Because of this, you are now able to
have your fruit to holiness and your eternal destiny can be everlasting
life."

My mind wandered back to the verses I read the other night. What
he had just said sounded so familiar. As I was wondering these things, he
took my hand and said, "Don't you know? You are a slave to what you
allow to control you, whether it be to sin leading to death, or obedience
leading to righteousness (rephrased from Rom 6:16, 18)."

"What can I do to repay you? I would do anything for you," I told
him. I felt so indebted to Him and grateful for my freedom from Sin.

"My dear child, follow me where I lead you and love me with all
your heart." (See Deuteronomy 6:5)

Right then and there I decided in my heart that no one was more
worthy of my life than this Jesus, so I surrendered everything to Him. I
gave my life to Him and yielded myself to Him as a willing "slave of

righteousness." Now, my greatest desire is to love Him for the rest of my life, all because He first loved me (1 Jn. 4:19).

Pulling this allegory back to listening to our parents' counsel, Jesus has commanded us to honor our parents. When we don't honor our parents, we do not honor or obey God either. In addition, many times, what our parents want us to do is really the right thing to do. Their counsel, if followed, can keep us away from that "old, oppressive ogre named Sin" and help us live a free life in Christ, even if they aren't Christians, and even if they don't follow their own advice. Don't reject their advice. Instead, think about it, pray about it, and find out how to honor God by listening to them.

Toolkit

-Lie: My parents' counsel is invalid because they don't follow it either. -

- John 13:15
- Romans 6:15-18
- Proverbs 28:14

Lies About Myself

My parents don't love me.

One woman shared with me that when she was growing up, she didn't feel any positive affirmation from her father. She remembers two hugs from her father - one as an 18-year-old and the next at her wedding.

It was hard for this woman to feel like her father was pleased with what she did. For example, she liked to run track in high school. One time she even won a bronze medal. But still, her father only offered her tips for improvement in place of praising her.

These events caused her to believe that she wasn't loved. These "unloved" feelings were pretty awful, but when she became a Christian, she allowed God to change her "unloved" mentality and realized that *God loved her*. Soon, she started reaching out to her dad with kind and caring words. For her, showing her dad the love that she missed from him helped bring healing to their relationship.

Another woman shared with me that she only remembers two times when her father told her he loved her. The first time was after a tragedy in her life. This lack of love was a struggle for both her and her siblings.

Both of these women had years of "unloved" trials as young adults, yet through their relationships with God, both have now moved on to know and love the Lord. Through their love for God, they have been able to reach out to people from which they felt little to no appreciation. In addition, they were also able to learn how to show love to their spouses and children. God's love was the answer to their problems.

As Christians, it is important to find our identity (what we believe ourselves to be) from Christ, and not necessarily from our parents. Even children with the best of parents can be disappointed and feel unloved at times, but Christ's love trumps all. Even though circumstances that surround may be unlovely, turbulent, and sad, Christ is still the great I Am and is sufficient for all our needs (2 Cor. 12:9). That fact doesn't change.

> "The Lord has appeared of old to me, saying: 'Yes, I have loved you with an everlasting love; therefore with loving-kindness I have drawn you.'" Jeremiah 31:3

Toolkit

-Lie: My parents don't love me. -

- Philippians 4:13
- Jeremiah 31:3
- 2 Corinthians 12:9
- List some nice things your parents have done for you.

I don't make my parents happy. I can't do anything right.

This is a lie that I fell into especially as a younger teen. I wanted so badly to please my parents that anything negative, such as a rebuke or a harshly worded statement, would leave me crying and hurt. This sensitivity even got in the way of my doing what made my parents happy! Whoops!

Was it bad that I wanted to please my parents? No. The bad thing was that I let my world revolve around what I thought would please them and allowed my joy to be affected when I wasn't able to receive the response I wanted. My desire should have been to please Christ *first,* then let my love for my parents and others follow. That has been a learning process for me. What helped me the most through this struggle was a simple verse my Dad shared with me. I hope it will encourage you, too.

"Or do I seek to please men? For if I still pleased men, I would not be a bondservant of Christ." Galatians 1:10b

When we try to please people, we are often focused on ourselves, what we are like, and what people think of us. Then, sometimes, we may take people's responses personally and can allow our lives to become negatively affected. However, when we focus on serving God and being a blessing to others, there is a freedom and joy that doesn't come without that focus. If we allow pleasing Christ to become more important to us than pleasing people, we will be able to have a joy that prevails even in the midst of difficult situations because of our focus on Christ.

Toolkit

-Lie: I don't make my parents happy. I can't do anything right. -

- Galatians 1:10b
- Hebrews 12:1-2
- List your accomplishments.
- List how you have helped others.
- Find out what Jesus wants you to succeed at.

Good relationships with my siblings are not important.

Having good sibling relationships helps create a loving atmosphere in the home. Whose parents wouldn't want that? The extent to which there is fighting, or lack of fighting, in the home will affect your parents' emotions. When there is less arguing and tension, it will be easier for them to show the love they have for you and your siblings.

You also want to pursue good sibling relationships to show your siblings how much you love and appreciate them. Your brothers and sisters need someone who will love them, enjoy them, and be with them. That person could be you if you take the time and make room in your heart! You will have your siblings around for the rest of your life, so you might as well make the most of your chance to cultivate a good relationship now!

Despite the many benefits of good sibling relationships, sibling relationships are difficult, oftentimes more difficult than parent relationships. Sometimes, as we try our best to work on a good relationship with them, it seems as if the battle will never be won. We need to remember that God often waits on us to give the battle into His hands before He allows us to experience victory so that *He* can be victorious in our lives. There have been many incidences in my life where I have waited on God, waited on God, and waited some more until I would finally break down and say, "God, whatever You want to happen is fine with me." Then, usually, something good has happened shortly afterwards (like the same day), and I've laughed at myself for not thinking about surrendering the situation to God earlier. However, I don't want to make you expect immediate responses after you take certain steps; it's no recipe. I really want to encourage you to keep seeking God in your life and to be expecting Him to fulfill His promises to you faithfully! (See chapter 10 for more on sibling relationships).

"So he answered and said to me: 'This is the word of the Lord to Zerubbabel: 'Not by might nor by power, but by My Spirit', says the Lord of hosts.'" Zechariah 4:6

Sibling relationships are tough and take hard work and perseverance, but they are definitely worth it. Not only for the sake of a peaceful home, but also for the sake of friendship, comradery, and fun. Close siblings have *lots* of fun together. You may think you have more important things to do than invest in your siblings, but as I've heard it said, people don't lie on their death beds wishing they had spent more time at work, in the gym, or having fun. What's normally most important to them is the people who have become part of their lives - people like your mom, your dad, your siblings, and your close friends! No matter what your family is like, if you have a family, you are <u>blessed</u>. Some people don't have any family at all. Make the most of it. Choose to make them an important part of your life.

Toolkit

-Lie: Good relationships with my siblings are not important. -

- Psalm 133:1
- Zechariah 4:6

I'm too young to do anything for God

After you read this section, you're probably going to think, "Anyone can do this! I want to do something *extraordinary*!" However, I happen to be convinced that the extraordinary has to begin somewhere and that "somewhere" is found in loving God, loving others, and being all God means for you to be <u>now</u>. There are small ways you can make a big difference. Your smile is unique to you. Use it as often as possible! Your loving presence and acts of kindness can make someone's day. There is something about *you* that is special. You can do things that no one else can. There are quadrillions of ways to use your life in service to God and others. In addition, at this young age in your life, you can learn good habits like prayer, Bible reading, and Bible memorization. If you are faithful in the little things now, God will be able to say later, as the master said to his servant in a parable Jesus told, "Well done, good servant; because you were faithful in a very little, have authority over ten cities" (Lk. 19:17). Keep that in mind.

If you're feeling like the little things you can do are "very little," you should take heart, because through faithfulness, your very little can grow into much! To put the above verse into math terms, a "very little" multiplied by faithfulness led to authority over ten cities. Wow! God's method of multiplication is very generous. Could you imagine *actually* being given ten cities? Maybe it won't be an actual "ten cities" in our lives, but, we should be encouraged. God is faithful to reward those who follow Him humbly and faithfully. It may not be immediate, in the way were imagining, or in the time frame we were expecting, but God does it in His own perfect way. Just stay surrendered to His will and seek His glory before everything else.

Some Ways you can Serve God Now

1) Obey your parents (Eph. 6:1)
2) Serve the Church (Rom 12:4-9)
3) Pray for laborers for God's harvest (Mat. 9:38)
4) Love God (Lk. 10:27)
5) Let your light shine (Mat. 5:16)
6) Encourage friends to love God (Mat. 28:19)
7) Be joyful – smile and sing praises (Phil. 4:4)
8) Work on character development (Col. 3:12-15)
9) Develop a heart to help others (Jas. 1:27)
10) Bring the requests of others before the Lord in prayer (Eph. 6:18)

"Then said I: 'Ah, Lord God! Behold, I cannot speak, for I am a youth.' But the Lord said to me: 'Do not say, 'I am a youth,' For you shall go to all to whom I send you, and whatever I command you, you shall speak... for I am with you to deliver you,' says the Lord." Jeremiah 1:6-8

Toolkit

-Lie: I'm too young to do anything for God. -

- Luke 19:17
- Matthew 6:33
- Jeremiah 1:6-8

I am not capable of what my siblings are capable of. I am less valuable than others around me. My family would be better without me.

A family is like a body. Each family member has different gifts, different interests, and different talents. In the same way, each of our body parts do something unique. Our feet help us walk; our hands help us eat, write, and touch; our brain helps us think and control our bodies. It would be silly for our body parts to compare themselves with each other because they are all beneficial to our life and health. We humans compare ourselves to other family members and people in our lives too often.

I have compared myself with other people many times throughout my life. If you've been considering comparison as a hobby, I definitely don't recommend it. Not only did it "drill holes" in my joy bucket, but it also made me less capable of serving others and doing certain things that would have benefited myself, my family, and the Lord.

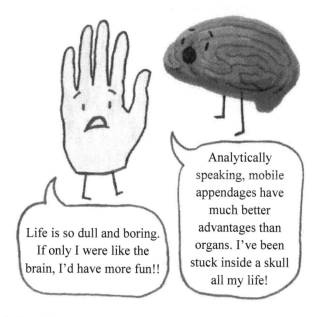

Life is so dull and boring. If only I were like the brain, I'd have more fun!!

Analytically speaking, mobile appendages have much better advantages than organs. I've been stuck inside a skull all my life!

So, next time you're tempted to view yourself as a less valuable or non-valuable family member, remember that if your hands and your brain are both important for daily life, you are also valuable to your family. God has given you special gifts that He hasn't given anyone else! You have a *unique purpose* to fulfill in life. Without you, your family would look like a puzzle with a missing piece. God desires that you trust Him and diligently pursue His will so that He can help you be amazingly helpful as you meet the needs around you that you are designed to help meet.

"For I know the thoughts that I think toward you, says the Lord, thoughts of peace and not of evil, to give you a future and a hope." Jeremiah 29:11

Toolkit

-Lie: I am not capable of what my siblings are capable of. I am less valuable than others around me. My family would be better without me. -

- Jeremiah 29:11
- 1 Corinthians 12:12-27 (This is a more in-depth illustration about the importance of each person as compared to body parts.)

Serving my family at home is not an eternal investment.

I really wish that I would have realized how many things I could have been doing for the Lord at home when I was younger. I somehow got this strange idea that "real ministry" was going overseas or doing something phenomenal with my life. That misconception distracted me from seeing all that God had in store for me at home. I missed the big picture, and that made it easy for me to think that I had to wait to have "these requirements done" or be "so old", etc. before I could be "useful" for the Lord. Since I was distracted from serving God, I didn't serve Him actively when I was younger and wasted much precious time.

When the Lord hasn't opened a door for you to do something "important," it may be that the "important" thing God wants you to do is sitting right under your nose. For me, those important things were ministering to my siblings and the girls around me. Sometimes you have to think outside the box. For example, at one point, I really wanted to start a girls' Bible study, but our life was too busy to add in another activity. So, instead of the Bible study, I ministered to younger girls I met at Christian gatherings and conferences by writing them letters of friendship and encouragement. I still do that now and it is a real blessing. Now, the Lord has blessed by opening doors for me to be involved in two different Bible studies, one for girls and one for college students! Ask the Lord to open your eyes to see what He may have in store for you. God can use the time you have in your youth to prepare you to serve Him better later as He did with me.

> Could it be that the important thing God has for you to do is waiting right in front of you??

When you think about it, many successful missionaries began their lives of service by being faithful at home. For example, young Hudson Taylor had known that God wanted him to go to China since his late teen years, but in his early twenties, he was still living in his home country. Despite his longings to go serve the Lord in China, he wisely spent his time at home preparing himself for the difficulties he could possibly experience in China later. He studied Chinese, lived primitively, budgeted, learned about the Chinese culture, developed a heart to reach their spiritual needs, and supported himself as an apprentice medical assistant. He also studied the Bible, prayed, and involved himself in various ministry outlets. His time in his homeland was not wasted.

It was years after Hudson felt the Lord's leading to go to China before the Lord opened a door for him to go. After finally arriving in China, Hudson was very grateful for what he had learned during his years of preparing for missionary life. He was able to use his studies of the Bible, Chinese, and medicine on the mission field. Do you see how he was being faithful in little things before God moved him on? He didn't waste his life when "nothing was happening," but instead, saw the value and richness of his youth and jumped at the opportunity to use those precious years for God as much as he possibly could[4].

"Let no one despise your youth, but be an example to the believers in word, in conduct, in love, in spirit, in faith, in purity." 1 Timothy 4:12

In Hudson's life, serving God at home was an eternal investment, as it can be in our lives as well if we allow it to be! So often, Satan can distract us from what is really important by making something else look more attractive or significant. We need to accomplish things with our lives, for God's sake, our sake, and the sake of others. However, accomplishment rarely just "happens." That's why we need to be faithful in little things. Even though our family may seem like a "little thing" in our lives, it is foundational and wise for us to invest our time and effort into these special people now while we have the chance.

---

[4] Summarized from *The Spiritual Secret of Hudson Taylor* (Written by: Dr. & Mrs. Howard Taylor)

Toolkit

-Lie: Serving my family at home is not an eternal investment. -

- Luke 16:10
- 1 Timothy 4:12
- Proverbs 12:27
- Proverbs 22:29

Do you See?

Have you noticed how many of these lies we have discussed are not beneficial to the person believing them? Good! I'm glad! I pray that God gives you the grace you need to conquer any beliefs that are contrary to His will and harmful to yourself as you walk forward in His glorious truth, uncovering lies and half-truths and ridding of them!

"Then Jesus said to those Jews who believed Him, 'If you abide in My word, you are My disciples indeed. And *you shall know the truth, and the truth shall make you free.*'"
John 8:31-32

"...the devil...*does not stand in the truth,* because *there is no truth in him.* When he speaks a lie, he speaks from his own resources, for he is a liar and the father of it." John 8:44

Open or Closed?

"If we confess our sins, He is faithful and just to forgive us our sins and to cleanse us from all unrighteousness." 1 John 1:9

All of our lives are already open and completely seen before God, but, somehow, we like to think that we can hide things from God, like Jonah did. Jonah was a man who *thought* he could be sneaky enough to run away from God (Jonah 1:2-3), but he found out the hard way that God *always* sees everything.

"You-Are-the-God-Who-Sees..." Genesis 16:13

It is good for us to tell God everything, big or small. It's not that He needs to know what we've done, He already knows. He sees everything. It's that we need to practice repentance and godly sorrow, reminding ourselves of Christ's forgiveness towards us. Confession also helps us remember that we have chosen to hate sin instead of embracing it. This action of transparency helps us and others see that we don't wish to keep sin in our lives anymore. Repentance marks the turning over of a new leaf.

Before going to our parents with worries, issues, guilt, or even just for counsel, we should always go to God. Even though God works through authorities (like parents) for His purposes, He ultimately wants a personal relationship with each of us. He wants us to seek Him so He can be a greater part of our lives (Jn. 15). Many times, we don't see Him working in our lives simply because we don't ask Him to!

"Yet you do not have because you do not ask." James 4:2b

Why should I be transparent with my parents?

We seem to have good reasons for hiding things from our parents sometimes, but are our reasons really all that great?

One thing I like to practice with my parents is honesty. That is, always telling them the truth, no matter how painful. It's almost always hard for me to share my struggles or my sin with my parents. I think this difficulty stems partly from a natural fear and reluctance to pull things out from my life into the open where others can see who I truly am, and partly because of fear of how they might respond to what I share. In the end, our relationships are stronger and my character is strengthened, though.

It's important to stay open and honest with our parents. Transparency is beautiful when kindled between parents and children, and it is so essential for children to live their lives in a way in which their parents are included. Lack of transparency, or hiding things, puts a wedge in the middle of the good relationship I know you want to have with your parents.

What to Share

Hidden Sins – Many times, when a sin is hidden, the person hiding it will know exactly what it is. At other times, this hiding is not so obvious to the person hiding it. In my life, I've noticed that I may not know when I'm hiding something because I've become immune to my own conscience. In these cases, my sin is subtle and unnoticeable to myself until my parents, or someone else, is around and I feel like hiding what I'm doing. This feeling of "hiding what I've been doing" is a warning to me. It's like a huge flashing yellow light which lets me know that what I'm doing is wrong.

Mom, Dad, I want to talk about something.

Perhaps the hardest part of bringing hidden sins into the light is getting over the fears that accompany confession. Please remember that the path of sin leads to death and that righteousness, although harder to come by, bears the sweeter fruit of righteousness! (See Romans 6:16+23)

Struggles – If there are things in your life that are just really bugging you, it might be a good idea to go talk with your parents. It may be something that is obvious to them or something that only you know about. Your parents will probably really enjoy the fact that you're coming to them for counsel and advice, and feel blessed, whether or not they let you know. Not many children go to their parents for advice! You can make them feel like one in a million.

Sometimes it's kind of awkward to share our struggles because we think that maybe we shouldn't be struggling the ways we are. The truth of the matter is that everyone struggles and needs to have people to talk to. Your parents were your age at one point. They probably have valuable advice to share with you! If you don't feel like you can talk to your parents about it your struggle, you may need to consider finding someone else to talk to. Remember this verse:

"No temptation has overtaken you except such as is common to man; but God is faithful, who will not allow you to be tempted beyond what you are able, but with the temptation will also make the way of escape, that you may be able to bear it."
1 Corinthians 10:13

How Open?

I used to be hypersensitive about having a clear conscience. I'd apologize for the sin of pride, then not long afterward confess how selfish my thoughts had been, and then still worry about what else there might be that I'd need to confess to someone else about. As you could imagine, that got annoying for my family after a while. Now, when I realize my weaknesses, I confess them to the Lord and ask Him for ability to change in those areas.

Usually, when a person feels like they need to confess sins too often, it's because of fear and insecurity. True, we are sinners and therefore sin daily, but there is a balance between healthy confession and hyper-confession. Insecurity happens when we turn our eyes inward on ourselves. We are sinful and depraved. There is nothing righteous in us (Rom. 3:10-20, Isa. 64:5-8). But Christ made us righteous and holy in God's sight through His blood.

"For all have sinned and fall short of the glory of God."
Romans 3:23

If I am righteous before God because of Christ, why would there be any need to be transparent? We need to be transparent because of the "old man." The "old man" is the part of us that still sins. The "new man" is what happened when we were born again in Christ (1 Pet. 1:23) and is incorruptible, being "...created according to God, in true righteousness and holiness" (Eph. 4:24b).

Our heart is like a house. God moved in, but our old self is just taking a while to move out. Meanwhile, we should strive, as Romans 12:2 says, to "...be transformed by the renewing of your mind..."

The reason it is so important to stay open with our parents and/or other believers is because the old man in us loves the world's ways, not God's ways. It hurts when part of the "old man" in us has to move out, and we don't like pain. So, we're tempted to hide him in our hall closet under something that will conceal the fact he's there. Wise people in our lives can help us get rid of him.

"But you have not so learned Christ, if indeed you have heard Him and have been taught by Him...*that you put off...the old man* which grows corrupt according to the deceitful lusts, and be renewed in the spirit of your mind, *and that you put on the new man...*" Ephesians 4:20-24a

Satan, the world's most skilled deceiver, also loves the ways of the flesh. Together, the "old man" and Satan make dangerous accomplices. By asking God to help us pull the deeds of our "old man" into the light, we're able to diminish Satan's power, have the "old man" move out, and give God room to work in our lives. Not only that, but we'll also be able to have sweet fellowship with other believers, not only because of shared struggles, but also because of nearness to Christ.

"But if we walk in the light as He is in the light, we have fellowship with one another, and the blood of Jesus Christ His Son cleanses us from all sin" 1 John 1:7

Don't Share it!

Recently, a friend of mine was offended by something her parents did. Their family was having a hard day. So, she went to a spare room and folded laundry to surprise her mom. When her parents found out her wonderful secret, the girl started crying. She and her mother made amends for what had happened. Then, she went to her dad for the purpose of reconciliation. After sharing some thoughts with her dad, the girl felt like her dad was defending himself. So, she told her dad, while she was upset, "This always happens! Whenever I try to be open with you I always feel like you just defend yourself."

My friend did not feel like her father was trying to understand her point of view, but instead, that he was standing up for his own perspective, which hurt her feelings. Even so, insulting comments should not have been communicated. No matter how wrong she thought her dad was, she should have still approached him in honor as a fellow person, treating him the way she wanted to be treated. The above story is a perfect example of one circumstance where people should not be 100% transparent with their parents! Meaning that we should be thoughtful and gracious in the way we share our feelings so that our parents are encouraged by our attempts to build a stronger relationship with them.

> "And just as you want men to do to you, you also do to them likewise." Luke 6:31

When to be Transparent with your Parents

- When your parents ask you to be transparent
- When you've lied
- When you feel let down (be *very* respectful!)
- When you're inwardly bothered by something
- When you feel discouraged and desire wise counsel
- When you are hiding something
- After you pray and ask God for wisdom and guidance

When not to be Transparent with your Parents

- When you're angry
- When you have a negative attitude
- When you want your parents to pity you
- When you're ungrateful for what your parents have already done
- When you want to have your own way

Spirit of the Conversation

We're going to briefly discuss five ways we can make touchy conversations with our parents more successful.

Gratefulness vs. Ungratefulness

"Mama," I queried, "When one of your kids comes to you for advice or help, what type of attitude would you not appreciate?"

"Selfishness or ungratefulness," she responded almost immediately.

We need to guard against selfishness and ungratefulness. People who focus on themselves tend to be "takers" instead of "givers." We need to be careful not to be like the leeches' daughters in Proverbs who cried, "Give! Give!" (Prov. 30:15).

Viewing our parents and their advice as special would be a good way to start being more others-centered in our relationship with our parents. Not every child has parents. Realize how blessed you are to have the parents you have, no matter who they are. Don't take their efforts for granted! They will be imperfect, so seek out positive qualities in them and make an effort to be grateful for those things!

Gratefulness has been defined as: "Making known to God and others in what ways they have benefited my life."[5] There are many ways to display gratefulness.

Gratefulness Tips:

1) Say "I love you!"
2) Thank them after advice. (Whether or not you think it was helpful at the moment.)
3) Recognize things they do for you with a joyful, "Thank you!"
4) Give them genuine smiles.
5) Praise them for positive character qualities.

Christ-Centeredness vs. Selfishness

At one point in my life, I had so many things in my life I wanted to work on that I kept going to my parents for advice over and over and over again. In some ways, it was necessary and good that I was open with them, but in other respects, I could have done better at focusing on their needs and the needs of others around me. I think if I would have focused more on others, I would have been happier, more fulfilled, and probably even growing more.

I read a prayer recently in Ray Comfort's *Evidence Bible* that starts out like this: "Father, I have a problem..." Before the person went on and shared his problem with God, he decided to pray for the many people who were less fortunate, dying, starving, homeless, sick, lost in sin... and his list went on and on. He really took some time, prayed from his heart, and spent the bulk of his prayer asking God to help each people group

---

[5] IBLP "Operational Definitions of Character Qualities" from IBLP

through their difficult situations. By the end of his prayer he said, "Strange. I can't seem to remember what my problem was..."

As this prayer shows, sometimes we allow our problems to overtake us and weigh us down unnecessarily. By doing so, we allow the "old man" to lead instead of Jesus. This chokes out our effectiveness in ministry and blinds us from being able to see and meet the needs of others. The path of selfishness leads the opposite way of the path of Christ. Even though the path of Christ is hard and uphill, it will ultimately lead to joy. Did you know that it is more fun to serve God and others than yourself? Oh boy, have you got adventure in front of you!! As Psalm 16:11 says so fittingly, "You will show me the path of *life*; in Your presence is fullness of joy; at Your right hand are pleasures forevermore."

Humility vs. Self-Righteousness

Openness with parents must always be approached with a humble heart and readiness to admit wrong. Otherwise, we will make our relationship with our parents tense because we stubbornly insist on holding onto an argument. We must be willing to admit we are wrong, or at least that we could be wrong. And if we admit to a sin or are found out in sin, but then justify it, we have done more harm for ourselves than good. Really, self-justification does very little for us, because in doing so, we are trying to make ourselves look better in order to hide the fact that we sinned. That's like breaking a bone and then pretending it isn't broken it so we can continue doing what we like to do. But, that would only cause more pain and take more time to heal. Likewise, sinning and then covering it up would be more painful and make that sin harder to remove from our lives than it would have at first.

"If we confess our sins, He is faithful and just to forgive us our sins and to cleanse us from all unrighteousness. If we say that we have not sinned, we make Him a liar, and His word is not in us." 1 John 1:9-10

Here's an example of how carrying a humble disposition is the better option for all of us:

One day, Sarah borrowed her dad's laptop without permission. Later, she felt kind of guilty about it, so she decided to "confess." She knocked on her dad's office door, and after he responded, she peeked her head around the wall, saying, "Hey Dad, I know you don't like people using your computer without asking first, but I *really needed* it for my school assignment earlier today, and, well, I thought you wouldn't mind, so I used it. Thanks!" With that, Sarah shut the door and walked away.

Okay...wow. That sounded like she almost confessed and then chickened out at the end. If you've *done* something wrong or <u>think</u> that *maybe* you did something wrong, go ahead and give it an all-out confession. Fortunately, Sarah rethought her apology, prayed, and went back to her dad later that night for confession round two.

"Dad, I borrowed your laptop today without asking. I should have asked your permission first. I am *so* sorry. I'm also sorry for the disrespectful way I talked to you about this earlier today. I acted like I didn't care about your feelings, and that wasn't nice of me. Will you forgive me?"

The second apology received a better response. The first time, Sarah's Dad felt disrespected, and worse, he got the idea that Sarah wasn't sincerely sorry! He may have even expected, subconsciously, that she would make the same type of unpleasant "confession" again in her future. However, the second time through, his response was much less awkward, and he appreciated her sincere confession. After the second confession, he said, "I'm so glad you let me know. Yes, of course I'll forgive you!"

"Thank you, Daddy! I love you," Sarah said with a hug.

"Thank you, Sarah. I love you too," her dad replied.

Sometimes apologies tumble out in crazy messes that don't sound all that great. Sometimes, we can come across short and terse, causing what we wanted to be a sincere apology sound insincere. In those cases when you've been misunderstood as being insincere in your apology, pray, ask gentle questions, and stay humble! Remain encouraged, because humility always comes before honor (Prov. 18:12). Practice makes progress!

Confidence vs. Fear

I nearly always run into fear when I need to confess something. When I was in my early teens, I had battles with fear, not just about talking with my parents, but about a lot of different things.

I had fears about whether or not my parents really wanted to hear what I had to say, even though they told me that they really did! I had fears about telling my parents what was going on in my heart. I had fears about my life and what it was going to be like. I had fears that my parents wouldn't love me if I told them about the thoughts that were circling through my head. And the list went on and on and on.

The good news is that fear can be trodden out when the light of God's Word is shone on it. I'm here to prove it! I learned through my struggles that it is always good to share with others what I am fearful of, because oftentimes the fears I have don't make sense or are contrary to Scripture.

An easy example is the fear of rejection. When people are afraid that others will reject them, they naturally pull themselves away from others because they believe they aren't good enough. Naturally, that also makes it harder for other people to enjoy their company. Now, that fear doesn't make much sense anymore, does it? People always like people who like them!

Another example is the fear of failure. Does God expect us to fail? No! He says "Yet in all these things we are more than conquerors through Him who loved us" (Rom. 8:37). Did you hear that? We are not only "conquerors," but *more than* conquerors in Christ! His Word also says, "I can do all things through Christ who strengthens me" (Phil. 4:13).

The apostle Peter had fear, too. Remember how he bounded out of the boat in in response to Jesus' command, walking on the water, full of excitement to be with Him (Mat. 14:22-33)? However, when Peter started to fear the storm surrounding him, he sank in the waves. I'm sure Jesus *could* have given Peter enough grace to go leaping and jumping to Jesus. But instead, Peter grew fearful, and therefore began to sink. Jesus had commanded Peter to come to Him on the water, so couldn't He have given Peter the strength needed to walk on the water as well? Why didn't Peter trust Him??

Peter's fear is what pulled him under water. Are your fears pulling you down? Are you going to sink as the storm overwhelms you, or are you going to look to Jesus while you walk <u>above</u> the waves? The storm is nothing to Jesus – He's the One who made everything! Let's trust Jesus. He controls the waves of life anyway.

"Let us lay aside every weight, and the sin which so easily ensnares us...looking unto Jesus, the author and finisher of our faith..." Hebrews 12:1-2

Fear is one of the most venomous arrows Satan has ever thrown. Thankfully, it's not something God has left His children defenseless against. Fear and faith are opposites. Fearfulness fights against faith and faith triumphs over fear. If we have a fear and start believing it, we invite it to work its deadly poison in our lives. Whenever we lift up the shield of faith in Jesus' name, we can quench the fiery darts of the evil one (Eph. 6:16).

> "When you make yourself vulnerable to your parents, be prepared to hear something that you may not want to hear. Your heart must be covered by the Word and prayer so that your response will be humble and you will have a willing heart to work things out. You see, your parents could be hurt too. They had no idea you were going to share your heart and they may react out of past hurts. Please be patient and have mercy on them. Feel their pain. Most importantly, think good things about them. Think thoughts about them like the Lord thinks about you: thoughts of love and kindness; thoughts of good and not evil; thoughts to prosper them."
> -Michele Normoyle (mother)

Transparency is something Satan fights hard against because it takes what Satan *could* nurture in darkness and exposes it to the freedom of God's light. If Satan can place fear in our hearts when there's something we want to share with our parents, he will try his hardest to keep it there so that we will be too afraid to share. We need to be confident that it is a good thing to talk about our concerns with *both* God *and* our parents. Fear, if invited to work its poison, can cripple one's heart and make it faint. Please pray about your fears and talk to your parents!

Continuance vs. Periodicity

Transparency is a huge blessing to those who have it because it opens opportunities for bonding and deeper relationships. It's hard to have a good relationship with someone you don't know! As you allow your parents to get to know you by being real and honest with them, your relationship will go to a whole new level. However, transparency is not a one-time deal. Windows are transparent, but they don't stay that way unless they are cleaned regularly. In the same way, our lives tend to get messed up and dirty here and there. Psalm 19:7 says that God's law turns us back to Him. As we read His Word, we can be reminded of what hurts the Lord and turn to Him instead of to the world. Keeping our life and attitudes open to our parents also helps keep us from straying from the Lord because our parents can often see problems we can't and warn us before it's too late!

The end goal of transparency is a close relationship with the Lord, but it just so happens that a good relationship with our parents and freedom are often some wonderful by-products! Complete freedom from sin can only be found in Jesus. Transparency alone cannot release us from its power. In fact, there are people who confess sins in vain because they so desperately desire to have the forgiveness that only Jesus offers. They live as spiritual invalids while Christ stands by holding out the grace and forgiveness they need for a victorious life. You, on the other hand, don't need to do that. You know that Jesus is standing by. Listen to Him!

"But it is good for me to draw near to God; I have put my trust in the Lord God, that I may declare all Your works."
Psalm 73:28

When Jesus died, He did a powerful thing for us. Our strong Savior defeated Satan, disarming him from all his power to harm us. Do you realize what that means? In Christ, Satan has no weapon against us because Jesus *disarmed him* and *triumphed* over him.

"'No weapon formed against you shall prosper...this is the heritage of the servants of the Lord and their righteousness is from Me,' says the Lord." Isaiah 54:17

"Having disarmed principalities and powers, He made a public spectacle of them, triumphing over them in it." Colossians 2:15

Hints to Detect a Lack of Transparency

It's helpful to know the "warning signs" that tell us we need to share a problem with a parent or another believer, and certainly the Lord. Here are a few examples:

- If you feel like you need to hide something (other than a birthday present!) when your parents walk into a room
- When you don't want to talk to your parents about something in particular
- When you sense in yourself a spirit of heaviness
- When you lack inner freedom
- When you are bitter or hurt
- When you are battling the enemy's lies
- When it's hard to read Scripture or pray

But I'm *Terrified*!!!

I don't know what happens when you go talk with your parents, but maybe it will help you feel a little better to know what happens when I share with mine. I nearly always cry. This is just me, but for example, recently, something happened between my parents and I that pained me. I was hurt and didn't even understand what I had done to cause them to say the things they did and act the way they

had. I was tempted to become bitter, but when I prayed and put the situation into the Lord's hand, Ephesians 5:9-10 came to mind and I realized that God didn't want me to sit in my sorrow, but to instead get up from my sorrow and find out what would please the Lord.

> "Walk as children of light...finding out what is acceptable to the Lord." Ephesians 5:8b+10

So, I walked into my bedroom where Dad was sitting on the couch helping my sister with school. I tried to hold back my tears as I explained my confusion and concern, asking him to help me understand why things went the way they had. As it turns out, I had misinterpreted my Mother's response after I came up behind my Dad to playfully scare him. She was having a hard time maintaining order with a sibling, and I was aggravating an already aggravating circumstance of which I was totally unaware! After Mom and Dad told me *that*, I felt so much better about my hurt feelings. Our relationship was restored and I was so grateful I had talked to them!

Fears about Transparency

There are many things that may be running through your head about transparency right now that I didn't touch on or don't even know how to touch on because I'm simply not in your shoes at the moment. Be comforted, though. We have an awesome God. *Jesus was tempted in every way so that He could sympathize with the trial you're going through right now.*

Go now and boldly approach His throne of amazing grace for your present needs (Heb. 4:15-16). After all, it will not be reading a book, saying a prayer, or even sharing with your parents that will really make your life better. It will be **Jesus** working through those things that will help. I wish I could explain, but He is simply unexplainable, so I'll leave the seeking and finding up to you.

> "And you will seek Me and find Me, when you search for Me with all your heart." Jeremiah 29:13

From the minds of others...

I talked to various young people about fears they have when they share things with their parents. I hope this list encourages you to know that you are not alone and that other people struggle with similar things you do. Here's what they said:

- They will make fun of me.
- They will be upset.
- I will get yelled at.

- They won't understand.
- I will get in trouble.
- They will tell others.
- They will think negatively about me.
- My life will be ruined or entirely different after I confess.

Strategy of Attack

Notice how all the fears mentioned in this list above are related to what people think of "me"? Proverbs 29:25 says, "The fear of man brings a snare, but whoever trusts in the Lord shall be safe." Also, Galatians 1:10 says "...Or do I seek to please men? For if I still pleased men, I would not be a bondservant of Christ."

There is a greater fear than the fear of man – it's the fear of the Lord! What is the fear of the Lord? "The fear of the Lord is to hate evil; pride and arrogance and the evil way and the perverse mouth..." (Prov. 8:13). This hatred of evil does not necessarily mean that you should hate those who do evil, but that you should definitely hate the presence of evil in *your* life. One way to hate evil is to expose it to the light by being transparent!

Even if we do get in trouble for confessing our sins now, we'll have more trouble from our sins the longer we hide or remain in them. Satan would love for us to keep our sins and fears inside, because then he is able to work more damage. He is not able to work in the light. Claim a verse from Scripture with which to fight fear (possibly Gal 1:10, 1 Pet. 5:8, or Jas. 5:16) and go forth in the strength and love of Christ!

Beyond Transparency

Something wonderful happens when your conscience is clear and sin cannot get in the way of joy anymore. You can look your parents in the eye, laugh harder at their jokes, and know that there is nothing that hinders God's hand of blessing on your life (Ps. 24:3-5). After a clear conscience and transparency comes friendship! Transparency is maintained by real, loving friendship. Friendship is fed by honor, love, and plenty of honest, down-to-earth conversations. Although transparency is hard work, in the long run, you will learn to enjoy cleaning the window of your life and being able to see the hand of God mightily at work[6]!

---

[6] I realize that a friendship with parents may not be possible, or immediately possible for people in every situation. Scripture is clear, we need to focus on walking in the light, independent of whether other people are or not (Eph. 5:8-10).

Baggage 101: Past and Present

"Therefore we also, since we are surrounded by so great
a cloud of witnesses, let us lay aside every weight...looking
unto Jesus..." Hebrews 12:1-2

Have you ever seen someone walking down the street with a
bag of trash just for fun? I'm guessing you probably haven't.
But, if you have, it probably looked
pretty weird. You would wonder
why they were dragging it around.
Maybe it was full of special broken
toys or trinkets that reminded them
of times in their life they didn't
want to forget. But...um...wouldn't
carrying it around everywhere get
kind of heavy and make life less
productive?

Do you ever carry around baggage? The baggage I'm referencing is the negative emotional memories that invade our lives, making relationships with those we love very difficult. Often, these hurts and sad memories are caused by the very same people we love so dearly, whether or not they know they hurt us. Do you carry any baggage in respect to past experiences with your parents?

The Nature of Garbage

How would you describe the trash in a garbage can? Stinky, smelly, icky, gross? Garbage is taken to trash cans *outside* of the house to be disposed of *far far away* because people know that they don't want garbage close by!

Oftentimes, bitterness over a situation can create a "stinky" attitude in us. We may not know we are carrying a bag of stinky trash, but it is often evident to those around us. Hurt feelings can rot away in a corner, and life's garbage bag continues to grow if not taken care of. Garbage is something we don't want to carry around. We should get rid of it.

How Baggage Accumulates

The "trash bag" where baggage accumulates is located deep inside you. When you decide to allow some word or circumstance to affect you negatively, you put the memory into storage there. Maybe you got upset about the way a parent harshly worded an instruction, or maybe you were ticked off because an authority made you feel like a baby again. Perhaps, someone mistreated you or did something to make your life less enjoyable. Might something like this still be bothering you now?

It's important to get rid of baggage, not only because it accumulates and gets heavy, but also because as current situations trigger us to remember past experiences, we tend to open our trash bags and pull out memories and live them over again in our minds. Maybe we do this because it makes us feel good. It is comfortable to us because we would rather keep our bitterness than go through the pain of removing it. However, when we choose to remain bitter about past experiences, we are, in essence, underestimating God's ability to work in our lives now, in the present. He can deliver us from our bitter baggage.

I thought that I smelled bad!

"But as it is written: 'Eye has not seen, nor ear heard, nor have entered into the heart of man the things which God has prepared for those who love Him.'" 1 Corinthians 2:9

Too often, we bring the past into the present by remembering past offenses. We expect people to act the same way they have in the past and react based off these memories. Because of this, situations often become worse. From my personal experience, most of the baggage I've carried has been the result of simple misunderstandings. Wouldn't it be awful if you were limping with a great burden to bear because of a simple misunderstanding! Wow, a lot of suffering for no reason! Still, misunderstandings do hurt. They may be hard, but they can also make your relationships stronger if dealt with in humility and love.

When we've been hurt by someone, we tend to build a wall of bitterness between ourselves and our offender. Why not, right? They hurt us, and in the back of our minds, we believe that they will probably do it again. We justify that we can't trust them anymore because of their past behavior and only expect to become more hurt if nothing is done to defend ourselves. <u>Stop</u>! Who is wanting us to

think that way? Jesus or Satan? Jesus wants to build us up, to give us joy and life abundantly. He also wants to bring blessings to those around us through our lives. But Satan will try to break up anything that could bring God glory.

The same way you may have baggage about your parents, your parents may have baggage about you. Because of this, it's really really *really* important to be humble, listen, and sincerely ask their forgiveness in areas you have been wrong. It will take time to work things out, but it will be worth it in the long run. Race to the foot of the cross in forgiveness. Ready? Set?? Go!!

"Yes, I have misunderstood my children and they have misunderstood me. This has been an opportunity for lies, like "Mom will never understand," to creep in. I tell my children that life at home is where we need to practice taking care of these "less-than-encouraging" situations. It does hurt and takes time and effort, but we will all be stronger in the future because of it. Home life, if viewed in a healthy way, can be a training ground for struggles and misunderstandings we will face outside the home."
— Michele Normoyle (mother)

Defining Bitterness

Bitterness is an unwillingness to forgive others. Even though you keep your garbage bag tightly closed, bitter thoughts often reveal themselves through hard faces, short comments, and strained relationships.

If nothing ever changes in your home so you can have a nice relationship with your parents, will you be angry and upset at them? Will you still choose to carry the baggage? Unfortunately, many people do. It drags them down, makes them angry, and wraps around them with sour memories that turn their faces into sour frowns. If you want to let go of your baggage, you need to do it, and do it soon.

Bye Bye, Baggage!!

So, what should we do? Should we go right away and let our parents know they have hurt our feelings?

Probably not. It takes sensitivity to the others' needs to find a good time to talk. If things are a little rough around the edges at first, start by building your relationship. Just enjoy their company and be kind and helpful. Later, when you're ready, ask your parents (or parent, depending on the situation) for a block of their time when they're not busy so you can talk with them.

A huge key to getting rid of baggage is forgiveness. Prayer makes forgiveness so much easier. It's hard to sincerely pray for a person we are bitter against (Lk. 6:28). Pray that God would bless them and show Himself to them. Pray that God would do things that only He can do. Ask Him to change their hearts. Ask Him to change *your* heart! Pray and watch as the hand of God does the unimaginable. Expect it. You are talking to a Person who is bigger than you, your parents, and your situation. He sees all the problems right off the bat. I wonder if He ever wonders when we're going to come to Him for help. He has given us all the grace we need to live a godly life (2 Pet. 1:3). All we have to do is rely on His grace and allow His strength to carry us through.

When Jesus taught us how to pray, He said, "...forgive our debts, as we forgive our debtors" (Mat. 6:12). Do we really want God to forgive us the same way we forgive others? I guess that's something to think about! What did we do to deserve God's forgivness? Nothing. What should others do to receive our forgiveness? Nothing. We don't sell our forgiveness. We forgive freely because we have been forgiven freely already by Christ (Mat. 10:8b).

Note: You can use letters or notes as a means of loving, relationship-building encouragement. Sometimes, I'll take a pad of sticky notes and write something encouraging (like something I appreciate about the person, a Bible verse, etc.) for my parents and siblings when no one's around. Then, after they're all in bed or out of the house, I'll sneak around and place them in obvious areas for the intended person to see. It's fun to be spontaneous like this. Plus, who doesn't love waking up first thing in the morning and seeing a loving note on their dresser, the microwave, or the door they exit?

If you need to talk with your parents about a situation that may be a misunderstanding, you could first apologize: "I'm sorry about what happened...I was not paying attention to your needs...I wasn't being as sensitive as I should have been...etc." Say whatever best fits your situation. If you apologize when you first approach them, you put the blame on yourself and eliminate some possibility of tension. After you have apologized, it *might* be ok to try and express how you felt when you were offended. Do it carefully, though! If due to the nature of the situation, you can only get so far as the apology and are not able to express your feelings, just be grateful you were able to apologize.

If you are able to express your feelings to your parents, avoid pointing fingers at them. When you express something negative you felt from them, you could follow it with something like, "I'm sure you didn't mean to make me feel that way, but it hurts and I'm not sure what to do about my pain. I'd like to hear that you love me and learn from you how I can do better next time." Conversations about misunderstandings can get touchy, so try to keep your tone gentle, kind, and sincere. Often people close up if they feel accused or mistreated, so do your best to show them love.

In some cases, it's impossible to speak to parents about personal things. In those cases, as in any case, we need to go to God in prayer. God didn't intend for us to carry baggage. In fact, He would much rather us carry around the news of His salvation to the world (Mat. 28:19-20)! When Jesus was on earth, He bore many burdens for our sake. For our sake, Jesus was tempted with the same temptations we are, yet was found without sin (Heb. 4:15). Now, Jesus offers Himself to become our Victory over baggage and sins in our lives. He wants to carry our baggage for us...

"Casting all your care upon Him, for He cares for you."
1 Peter 5:7

Deal with baggage right away!

Imagine living inside a castle and having an enemy yelling threats at you from outside the wall. The longer you allow him to taunt, the more time he has to build reinforcements. How long do you want your enemy the devil to be reinforcing bitterness in your life?

In Chapter 7, we talked about a type of baggage called lies. Lies can slow us down spiritually, emotionally, and even physically. It is helpful to write out the lies you are believing and go through them one by one with the goal of *disposal*. Chapter 6 would also be a good chapter to go back to if you need more encouragement on this.

Baggage can weigh people down easily. Instead of remembering all the negative things that have happened in the past, try to think of everything and *anything* positive to counteract the negativity. It may be helpful to write a list. Be thankful for how your parents provide for you, how they took care of you as a needy infant, and how they have directed you throughout your life. Remember the nice things they've done for your birthdays, the gifts they've given you on special occasions, or the things they've bought you just because. Do not focus on the pain or disappointments, but instead, find joy in *every little thing.*

"Love suffers long and is kind; love does not envy; love does not parade itself, is not puffed up; does not behave rudely, does not seek its own, is not provoked, *thinks no evil*; does not rejoice in iniquity, but rejoices in the truth; *bears* all things, *believes* all things, *hopes* all things, *endures* all things. Love never fails."
1 Corinthians 13:4-8a

How to Avoid Picking up Baggage

Get rid of your garbage bag!! Even if there's nothing in it and it's a lot lighter without all that nasty junk you've gotten rid of in it, there's still no reason to reserve a place in your heart where you allow yourself to store hurt feelings and emotions. Make no room for baggage in your life whatsoever. Oftentimes, we focus on selfish things and sink into a downward spiral. Reject the temptation! Use the following Scripture to combat your thoughts. In this verse, the word "lust" can be thought of as being anything your flesh would want to do, including keeping your garbage.

"But put on the Lord Jesus Christ, and *make no provision for the flesh*, to fulfill its lusts." Romans 13:14

It's important not to let negative thoughts and feelings linger. Ephesians 4:26b-27 goes even so far as to say, "...do not let the sun go down on your wrath, nor give place to the devil." This is an excellent synopsis of what we've been talking about! If we let the devil put his foot in the door even for a little bit, it won't be long before he comes in and wreaks havoc in some area in our lives! Command him to leave in the name of Jesus. Dedicate your life, your mind, your heart, your body, and your family relationships to Jesus in total surrender as you go forward in His might!

"Therefore we also, since we are surrounded by so great a cloud of witnesses, let us *lay aside every weight*, and the sin which so easily ensnares us, and let us *run with endurance* the race that is set before us, *looking unto Jesus...*"
Hebrews 12:1-2

Out of Love

True forgiveness is shown when we sincerely desire the best for our offender. For this to take place, it is important to have a relationship with Jesus. Because of the great love we have received from Christ, we can be driven to share the same love with others in a sacrificial, unconditional, and Christ-centered way.

> *Reach out just because of love. Not for gain, not for approval, not for fulfillment, but just because your love for Jesus has caused you to love them more and you want your life to prove that...then everything else will follow.*

Showing Christ's love often starts in very practical ways, such as sitting next to your parents, letting them know you love them, or asking them if you can do anything to help. Think about what makes your parents feel loved or special, and do accordingly. The "why" behind your action is the most important part of showing them love. Reaching out because you love them (not because you expect anything in return) will make the difference.

> "I have invested in my relationship with my parents by sharing my life goals, my desires, and the things God is teaching me and leading me to do with them. Since I know my mom's love language is quality time (this means she feels loved when people spend special time with her), I purpose to go places with her, tell her about books I am reading, and just talk with her about what is going on in my life." -Anna

I've heard it said that relationships are built little by little. It is not one amazing day that will make a difference, but years of little acts of love that build on each other. Those acts of love may be washing dishes, giving a hug, playing with siblings, saying, "Goodnight, I love you!" before bed, or tidying the house. Fun things and "work things" must be mixed in with each other. If you were only willing to do the fun and easy, like writing sticky notes or saying "I love you!" the relationship wouldn't be real. Love must be proven by the way you live your life every day (Jn.15:12; Heb. 12:3). Love sacrifices its own desires to meet the needs of others. So, have fun washing the dishes!

Extra Baggage

If you want to be a winner, you must travel light.

Round up all your extra baggage and throw it aside.

Good things can be bad things if they slow down your pace.

Ask the lord for strength and knowledge to finish the race!

Look to Jesus Christ your leader and leave weights behind.

Don't let Satan's baggage burden your body or mind.

Set the right example for the rest of the pack.

Throw away the worthless clutter that's holding you back!

Get rid of that extra baggage if you want to win the crown.

Get rid of that extra baggage 'cause it's sure to slow you down.

Just lay aside each weight; it's a villain in disguise!

Get rid of that extra baggage if you want to win the prize!

Friends and Siblings – How They Tie In

"And be kind to one another, tenderhearted, forgiving one another..." Ephesians 4:32a

This is a book about getting along with and honoring your parents. Part of that honor happens in accordance to your interactions with brothers, sisters, and friends. Isn't it natural for parents to want their children to have uplifting friendships? Wouldn't it be refreshing for them if you and your siblings started signing peace treaties instead of constantly picking fights?

When I was younger, I did a lot of this: "Uhg!! Siblings are sooo annoying!" I inwardly believed that things went sour because of siblings, and that there wasn't anything to do about it. I'm so grateful that I have gotten to watch families with really good sibling relationships, because they made me think that *maybe* siblings were actually worth some effort! I fought the good fight (the spiritual one, not the relational!) and worked to change my heart. Now I can say that my siblings are amazingly fun and a priceless blessing. I don't know what I'd do without them.

I remember when I was young, I started to play piano for family worship time. Given my new skill, I had to concentrate hard in order to play at all. Many times, I messed up and had to stop the song entirely! Unfortunately, there was barely a time I messed up and didn't think (and say) something like "So-and-so was standing too close!" or "So-and-the-other are singing too loud for me to concentrate!" (Notice how I was shifting my blame onto someone else and believing that it was their fault that I couldn't succeed?)

I could have been right a *few* times, but really, I should not have been focusing on how *others* could improve their singing or relational skills. That's prideful. Instead, I should have realized that God wanted me to come to Him about improving *my* skills. As time went by, God did teach me to do that. He also worked in my heart so that I could respond to irritations in a loving way. Now if my piano playing doesn't sound right, it isn't my siblings' fault anymore. (And are they ever happy!) I just know I should practice more.

Often, through negative thinking, we can "make" irritations out of siblings, like I did while playing piano. Next time your siblings irritate you, think about how your little (and big) brothers and sisters are a *huge* gift from God that you've really only begun to open. If you only had one more day with them, how would you use it?

We can also remind our siblings how wonderful they are and thus "make" blessings out of them. Recently at breakfast, one of my sisters complimented a brother on how gentlemanly he was acting. "Thank you!" he responded. Then, the unexpected occurred. She said she needed milk for her cereal and he exclaimed, "I'll get that for you!" Then, noticing that she still didn't have a drink, he got her a cup of water too. We both sat there stunned. See how powerful our words and actions can be?

The Not-so-Happy Sisters

One day I was writing in a small café attached to a local bookstore. As I was sitting there, my attention was drawn to two women, maybe in their late 50's, who looked like sisters. One woman picked up a phone and started talking. Not long after, I heard this irritated conversation that drew the attention of many in the room.

"Just give the phone to me!!"

"Ok! *OK!!*"

Even as a casual onlooker, I could tell that for some reason, their relationship was strained.

This incident reminded me of how important sibling relationships are. The reason I'm trying to build strong sibling relationships now is not so that I can just somehow *survive* my relationships with them (as the not-so-happy sisters were trying to do). I try to build strong relationships with them because I *love* them and I know that God has placed them in my life for a good reason. Brothers and sisters tend to stay in touch much longer than most friends. Family is one of those things that just seems to stick around, no matter what. Even those 50-year-olds in the café could attest to that! What type of relationships do you want with your siblings? Pray about it and take action to make it real![7]

Your siblings are as much a part of your parents' lives as you are. They are your parents' children, so it is important that you treat them well, not only for your parents' sake, but also to please the Lord. If you have siblings and are living at home, much of your parents' day-to-day interactions are with you and your siblings. You can play a part in giving your parents a gift that cannot be bought with money: a peaceful home. Is that not what you would want if you were a parent?

> God gave you siblings for a reason. We don't want to build strong family relationships simply to survive life at home, but to serve them and to live life to the fullest.

Living in an Understanding Way

You are different than each of your siblings. You process information differently and are affected by circumstances in totally different ways. Because of this beautiful variety, it may be hard to be sensitive to their needs 100% of the time. It's nothing that can't be worked on, though, right? The Lord's grace is always sufficient (2 Cor. 12:9). Maybe you should ask your siblings what *you do* that annoys them or how *they* would like to see *you* grow in character. Is there anything you do that

---

[7] Book referral: "Making Brothers and Sisters Best Friends" by Sarah, Stephen, and Grace Mally

they find annoying? Even if they say no, leave the door of your life open so they can tell you later if they need to.

I've noticed that sometimes it can be hard for older siblings to connect with younger ones, especially if there's a considerable age gap! Too often, older siblings push their little siblings aside as unimportant compared to their goals and schedule without realizing how much this can hurt!

I say this because I've done it before. I probably still have no idea how much what I do makes an impact on them. I am the oldest of six. My siblings want me to like them, love them, and approve of them. When I fail to make this happen, it hurts. I have really appreciated how my siblings have let me know in a loving way when I hurt their feelings so that we can work on our relationships and make it better!

If you are a younger sibling whose older sibling does not seem to have time for you, please realize that they may not even know that they are ignoring you and probably don't even want to do it! It will be a gift for them in the long run to know that they have a younger sibling who loves them and cares about the relationship! As we talked about in the chapter on transparency, every problem needs to be approached with respect, love, gentleness, and perseverance. Using harsh words builds road blocks where you want roadways for a stronger relationship.

Prayer Power

Prayer will change your world. You can pray for your siblings and consider them a "knee-worthy" ministry. If they know that you want to invest into their lives because you love them, they will learn to love you, too. They should know that you are not trying to change them, but that you are simply trying to be a better sibling. Find out what makes them smile. Discover what causes them to feel loved, and seek counsel from wise older Christians (perhaps your parents) if you encounter difficulties.

Here are some ways to be praying for yourself:

- Humility- This quality is vital. We know the result of pride is contention (Prov. 13:10). The opposite of pride is humility, and with humility comes graciousness and joy! When your siblings see you walking in humility, they will be more prone to listen to what you have to say (Jas. 4:6).
- Your love for Jesus – Pray that you will draw nearer to Christ and have a better understanding of how much Christ loves you (Eph. 3:18-19). The more we realize how much God loves us, the easier it becomes to show love to our siblings, and anyone God may bring across our path.
- Your love for others – Jesus commanded us to love each other in the same way He has loved us (Jn. 15:12). Love covers a multitude of sin (1 Pet. 4:8). Love is something each one of your siblings will need. Love also endures all things and perseveres

When the going gets tough, let the tough get loving!

(1 Cor. 13:7). Your siblings will need to see *you* show them love and grace even when *they* are hard to get along with. So, when the going gets tough, let the tough *get loving*! You could also ask God, your parents, and possibly even your siblings, to point out when you say or do something unloving. Unfortunately, we often don't know what we're doing wrong until someone tells us. So, it's good for them to let us know sometimes!

- Discipleship – Jesus commanded us to go and make disciples of every nation (Mat. 28:19). Fortunately for us, that doesn't have to mean draining our bank account to buy a plane ticket to Africa. A major part of our mission field is right in front of us – our siblings first (if we have them), and then others around us. Use your Bible to find out what discipleship means. Ask God to show you how you can practically show your siblings the love of Christ. Pray for them and reach out to them. Your work will by no means be fruitless (1 Cor. 15:58)!

Prayer Points for your Siblings:

- That God would be constantly at work in their lives.
- That they will be responsive to God's work in their lives.
- For any areas they may need to grow in character.
- That God would bless them as they accomplish their responsibilities and would help them do every task with excellence of spirit, serving the Lord (Col. 3:23).
- For their future job, ministry, spouse, etc.
- Pray some scripture verses for them such as Ephesians 1:15-21 and Colossians 1:9-14.

I also highly recommend asking them how *they* want you to pray for them!

Encouraging your Siblings to Honor their Parents

Have you ever heard the saying that praise given in front of others doubles and triples the effect? Some children speak badly of their parents openly before their brothers and sisters. Others openly speak well of their parents. It is honoring to speak well of your parents at all times. You have been given the opportunity to influence your brothers and sisters to honor their parents by speaking of your parents in a loving way in front of them.

You have an influential place in your family. It doesn't matter if you are first, third, or fifth born. You are influential. Why? Because *you* can encourage your family members to think well of themselves, *you* can set an example (to both older and younger siblings) of a strong walk with the Lord. *You* can lift a load on a cloudy day with a smile and hug. You can share a loving thought or give a helping hand. *You* can impact your family and *you* impact them every day, whether you know it or not.

Everyone is a leader. Some lead in righteousness, others in rebellion. Some lead in diligence, others in slothfulness. Some lead in joyfulness, others in grumpiness. When others see what you are doing, they will be more prone to do it as well because they have an example to follow – you! So, set a *good* example to your siblings, your friends, and those younger ones you haven't realized that look up to you at church, school, and the events you go to. *You* make a difference...really!

Ideas for how to have a positive impact on your siblings:

- Show excitement to honor your mom and dad. When there is a task they want done, do it cheerfully and with all your heart, as unto the Lord (Col. 3:23)!

- When doing things on a day-to-day basis, strive to live in an honoring way, both outwardly and inwardly. Come along side your siblings to remind them of what honors your parents and help them obey by setting a good example.
- Team up with a sibling to do a surprise for your parents, like cleaning a bathroom or doing the dishes. Something that is unexpected and kind.
- Pray for your siblings! It may be that not all of your siblings are at a place in their hearts where they *want* to honor their parents. Pray that God will give them that desire.

Friends and Parents

There are some things in life that only an older adult can see. One of those things might be the integrity of our friends, or their lack of integrity. Sometimes our parents can see things we can't. We could be having a grand time for all we know, but our parents are standing back biting their finger nails. Could it be that they knew all along that that particular friend wouldn't be the greatest? Don't wait to find out!

If your parents don't like your friends, it might be a good time to pray and relocate to another pool of friends. It's always a good idea to ask your parents for advice: "Dad, do you think Margret would make a good friend? Why or why not?" "Mom, do you think Daniel would be a nice person to get to know?" Their opinion is worth all the years it took them to form it. Listen up! It might just be the best thing you've ever heard.

Some friends might pull you away from what your parents want you to be doing or from the character they want you to develop. Some friends might have the attitude that parents aren't "cool." Some friends might be dishonest and disrespectful with their mouths. Those aren't the type of encouraging friendships you want to develop. 1 Corinthians 15:33 says that bad company will corrupt good character. The friends you have will ultimately shape who you become. Honor your parents and search God's Word for what He says about friendship. Here are some good verses for starters: Prov. 12:26, Prov. 27:17, Prov. 13:20, Prov. 18:24, Prov. 27:9, Prov. 27:6, and Prov. 22:24-25.

Honoring the Lord in our Friendships

Are you a friend who simply "hangs out" or do you actively point your friends towards the Lord? Do you make your friends interested in foolish things or do you encourage them to pursue Christ? Do you encourage friends to memorize random facts about famous people or do encourage them to memorize Scripture with you? Are you a friend who hides wicked deeds and does them behind your parents' or authority's backs, or do you come into the light and confess, fervently praying that your friends learn to do the same?

If you go back to the last paragraph, you could probably find many different types of friends hidden within and throughout the sentences, but when it all boils down, people can influence their friends in either right or wrong ways. This is such a sobering thought! Just think, one day we will have to give account to God for everything we have ever said or done (Rom. 14:12), and our friends will be part of that story. Are we going to use our friendships for God's glory?

In Real Life

Where does one find a wise friend? At a conference, I listened to a missionary's wife named Alissa share on the topic of friendships with a group of teenaged girls. She told about how when she was younger, she had two friends who were sisters. The three of them were very close and the best of friends.

One day, her friends pulled her aside at church and asked her to come out to the car with them. In the car, they told her that they couldn't be friends anymore. They explained plainly that they were going to dress a certain way and behave around boys differently than they knew Alissa would. Alissa asked, "Are you sure we can't still be friends?" They insisted that the friendship was over. Soon, they parted ways. This grieved Alissa deeply because she had been such good friends with them. Where would she find such deep friendships again?

The next couple years of her life, Alissa had a few friends, but nothing like she had before. Although it was hard, Alissa is grateful now for this "barren" season of friendship in her life. Do you know why? During those long years, she was able to rely on the Lord for friendship and deepen relationships with her parents and siblings. If she was always running around with friends, she probably would not have had this opportunity during the time it was most important. The Lord knew exactly what He was doing!

Years later, the Lord provided some wonderful, God-fearing friends for her through ministries she was involved in. These girls are still an encouragement to her now as a wife and mother. She is very glad that she waited on the Lord through that long, "barren" season of friendship. She is more blessed now because of it.

A Note on Friends

Friends are a powerful thing. Have you ever thought of them in that way? They influence your choices, impact your days, and will eventually chart your life in some way or another.

If you choose to walk with bad friends, chances are you will eventually walk down a bad path. If you choose to walk with godly friends, you'll be more likely to be on a godly path. It is so important to make sure that the people you are spending your time with will build you up and push you in the right direction.

"He who walks with wise men will be wise, but the companion of fools will be destroyed." Proverbs 13:20

How does this relate to honoring our parents? It goes back to Proverbs again, "The father of the righteous will greatly rejoice, and he who begets a wise child will delight in him" (Prov. 23:24). I think it's natural for a parent to rejoice when things go well for their children, wouldn't you think? When we do what is right, we honor our parents and make them happy.

Being a Good Friend

People need friends who will listen to them, who will encourage them and point them to the Lord. Do you have any friends like that? Are *you* that friend? Maybe the friends you have would be interested in doing a Bible study or praying with you over the phone once a week. Or maybe, they just need you to be praying for them.

Friends who really love the Lord are a treasure. They are a blessing through and through. Whether you are very blessed with good friendships or feel a need in your life to have more friends, I would encourage you to reach out, not necessarily looking for friends, but in *being a friend*. Who needs encouragement? Who needs prayer? Is there anyone who looks lonely? Can *you* be their friend? God made us with a desire to have friendships, but He also told us to "Go...and make disciples of all the nations" (Mat. 28:19). God wants us to share with others how Jesus has taught us to love Him and help them to love Him too. So, make some friends purely for the sake of meeting needs and showing them Jesus' love. They're probably waiting right under your nose, and perhaps even in your own family!

Tips for Building Up your Friends in the Lord

- Encourage them. Keep your eyes open for positive character qualities you have seen in them and let them know!
- Read the Bible and memorize Scripture together.
- Point to the Lord. Are they sad? Are they discouraged? Ask if you can pray for them, and pray for them often!
- Pray with each other. Is there a concern that needs prayer? You could even pray that God will give both of your parents wisdom and grace as they raise you! Drop to your knees with your friends! God can make wise friends wiser still.

Final Thoughts on Friends and Siblings

Friends and siblings are some of the most wonderful people in our lives. They are in our lives so we can encourage each other, help each other grow, and point each other to the Lord. One wonderful thing about godly siblings and friends is that they can help keep us accountable for living a godly life! You can do the same for them, too, by asking, "How has your walk with the Lord been?" "How can I pray for you?" "What was the most difficult part of last week?", "What was the best part the week for you?" etc. As your relationship with the Lord grows stronger, it will be easier to pray for others and know how to reach out in love. Our final goal should be to honor the Lord and our parents through the friendships we share with others.

The Best Friend of All

Even though there are a lot of nice people to be friends with, Jesus is the Friend above all other friends. He always knows how to comfort and help us when we need it. He never thinks an unloving thought about us (Jer. 29:11), and has set an example for love, saying, "Greater love has no one than this, than to lay down one's life for his friends" (Jn. 15:13). Although other friends can get busy and have things to do, Jesus is never too busy and we can always talk to Him about our thoughts, problems, and dreams. He says, "I will never leave you nor forsake you" (Heb. 13:5b). Jesus is such a good friend that the psalmist states, "When my father and my mother forsake me, then the Lord will take care of me" (Ps. 27:10).

By being our friend, Jesus does not stop being God, He just comes to amaze us at how such a holy and awesome God could love us enough to be our personal friend. On earth, Jesus was known as a "friend of sinners" (Lk. 7:34). He wants to be our friend and win our hearts. Remember how Hebrews 12:2 says, "Looking unto Jesus...who for the joy that was set before Him endured the cross..."? That "joy that was set before Him" was **you**. He finds joy in letting you enjoy the richness of His glory through your freedom from sin and life in Him.

"The Lord your God is in your midst, the Mighty One, will save; *He will rejoice over you with gladness*, He will quiet you with His love, *He will rejoice over you with singing*."
Zephaniah 3:17

God is someone we can trust. He is someone to lean on when we're weak, to go to when we're discouraged, and to stay with when we need shelter. He doesn't condemn or think badly of us (Rom 8:1). He's heard it all already. He understands what you're going through even better than you ever have or ever will. No friend, sibling, or parent can even begin to compare with our Savior. Even though relationships are great, Jesus is the greatest and we are so blessed to have a chance to know Him personally as our Lord!

Raising the White Flag of Victory

"For whoever desires to save his life will lose it, but whoever loses his life for My sake and the gospel's will save it. For what does it profit a man if he gains the whole world, and loses his own soul?" Mark 8:35-36

In the midst of a battle, if one side grows overwhelmed and needs to stop fighting, that side surrenders and gives the victory to the other army. A white flag is raised to signal the end of the battle. God wants us to win our battles in life, but He asks us to allow Him to win the battle through us.

Backwards Victory

What type of victory do you want? Do you want Christ to help you accomplish *your goals,* or do you want to surrender and allow God to accomplish *His goals* through you?

Often, our idea of victory is quite backwards. Sometimes we pray prayers that ask God for the victory *we want* and the ability to do what *we want to do.* I think God probably sits back sighing, wishing He can answer us - but He can't feed our flesh! Would a loving heavenly Father give us everything we want if He knows it's not good for us? No. God is good. He is more concerned about who we become than about what we get while reaching our goals. He wants us to become like Christ. In the long run, this will help us live more fulfilled lives.

"You lust and do not have...you ask and do not receive, because you ask amiss, that you may spend it on your pleasures." James 4:2a+3

According to Strong's Concordance, the word "amiss" in the above passage is translated "badly." So it could read like this, "you ask and do not receive because you ask *badly...*" Due to lack of an appropriate focus, we tend to ask for the wrong things. We need to raise the white flag of surrender in our hearts to Jesus and strive to learn how to pray how *He wants* us to pray. That is, we must pray about the things on our Father's heart: the lost, the hungry, the sad, the searching, your authorities, your family, and for Christ to be evident in your life - things that would benefit His kingdom!

Verses with topics to pray about: Matthew 6:9-13, 1 Timothy 2:1-2, Romans 10:1, Psalm 122:6, 1 Corinthians 1:4, Colossians 1:9-12, Ephesians 1:15-21, etc.

I've heard people pray like this before, saying, "Lord, *if it be your will,* please allow 'this thing' to happen." Jesus used these same words in the Garden of Gethsemane before going to the cross. He said, "Father, if it is Your will, take this cup away from Me; nevertheless not My will, but Yours, be done" (Lk. 22:42). When we pray for God's will to be done, we can start seeing miracles and answered prayer, and we will find:

"Yet you do not have because you do not ask." James 4:2b

How are you praying for your parents? Are you asking God to change their hearts so that they will buy you a toy or a car or let you go out with some friends? Or, would you rather God receive the glory through whatever happens, all the while letting God know your needs and desires (Phil. 4:6)? He wants our joy to be complete, but if He is constantly giving us all the material things we want, we will become distracted from the Source of true joy and fulfillment.

Surrender

What if God's best treasures are only found by walking through a fiery trial? What if God's idea of life is completely different than ours, but still so much better? What if the very people to whom we hold so dearly seem to be the hardest to get along with? What if our dreams become shattered when life unfolds itself?

"'For My thoughts are not your thoughts, nor are your ways My ways,' says the Lord. 'For as the heavens are higher than the earth, so are My ways higher than your ways, and My thoughts than your thoughts.'" Isaiah 55:8-9

Ok, so God's plans *are* better than ours. He sees the whole picture, including the past and the future. His thoughts *are* different than our thoughts. It would be kind of nice to have the "perfect lives" we imagine in our dreams, but could even our most treasured dreams compare with God's plans? Hmm...probably not. It may be that what you are going through with your parents is part of His perfect plan for you and will help you grow in Him.

Does God's "good plan" still count for you when every day under your roof is a scorching desert of relational tension and dismaying circumstances? How real that is. Part of God's answer for you is in the below verses:

"My brethren, *count it all joy* when you fall into various trials, knowing that the testing of your faith produces patience."
James 1:2-3

"In this you *greatly rejoice,* though now for a little while, if need be, *you have been grieved by various trials*, that the genuineness of *your faith*, being *much more precious than gold that perishes*, though it is tested by fire, may be found to praise, honor, and glory at the revelation of Jesus Christ."
1 Peter 1:6-7

Okay, that's a lot easier said than done. I have no clue what your situation with your parents is, but I do know that Jesus has promised to never leave you nor forsake you (Heb. 13:5). I also know that other people are going through similar struggles as you in their lives (1 Pet. 5:8-9). God admonishes us to rejoice in trials, and not just "rejoice," but also to "*greatly* rejoice." So, for all of us, when we are having a bad day or a troublesome time with our parents, instead of fighting back and being moody, we need to find something to be grateful for or simply just thank God in faith for how He is working everything out for good (Rom. 8:28), even though it may not be obvious to us yet.

Exchanged Trials

The question we need to consider is: What does God want me to do with these trials I have with my parents?

When we allow God to teach us through our trials, they can turn into "gold." This "gold" of strengthened faith and character, is much more precious than mere "gold that perishes" (1 Pet. 1:7). It is attained as people walk with Jesus through the fires of affliction, loneliness, tension, betrayal, poor health, family struggles, and the list goes on.

People who have been through difficult times and stayed faithful to Christ have so much to offer the world. They have so much wisdom and understanding to share about how to cling to Christ when the wind blows strong! They have learned little by little to give up what they desire and surrender their plans to God. They trust Christ amidst the storm and bring blessings to those around them, all the while glorifying the Lord.

God takes our hardest times, our trials, our struggles, and our temptations and makes them into something He can use. He only asks us to give them to Him. Yes, He can use even our worst days with our parents! As I mentioned earlier, God is gentleman, He does not force our compliance, even though He knows what is best. God requests to help us and then patiently molds us to the image of His Son, Jesus (Rom. 8:29). Maybe that's why building a relationship with your parents is taking such a long time. Maybe God wants you to surrender the whole thing to Him and trust Him with it!

With each trial you face, turn to face Jesus and ask Him to help you walk through it. Don't forget God's promises and cling to Christ with all your might! [8] Please, please do!!

> "He has sent Me to heal the brokenhearted...to give them **beauty for ashes**, the oil of joy for mourning, the garment of praise for the spirit of heaviness...*that He may be glorified.*"
> Isaiah 61:1b+3

> "*He also brought me up out of a horrible pit*, out of the miry clay, and *set my feet upon a rock*, and established my steps. *He has put a new song in my mouth* – praise to our God; many will see it and fear, and will trust in the Lord."
> Psalm 40:2-3

I'd Rather Have Jesus

> "He who loves father or mother more than Me is not worthy of Me. And he who loves son or daughter more than Me is not worthy of Me. And he who does not take his cross and follow after Me is not worthy of Me." Matthew 10:37-38

Don't take this verse wrongly. Is giving up on our parents what Jesus meant for us to do? Is that the way we're supposed to follow Him? By discontinuing obedience and love to our parents? No.

---

[8] Isaiah 54:10-17 is a really good passage for encouragement. It's so long that I didn't add it here. It's worth a read, though!

Family relationships are a really good thing, but if we put family relationships before God, it's idolatry. Idolatry happens when something takes the place of the Lord in our lives. What if we are never able to have the relationships with our parents that we wanted? What then? Will God still be God in our hearts?

I believe God is asking us to come to a place where we can say, "Yes, Lord, I'd rather have You than a really nice relationship with my parents." Even though it brings honor to the Lord when children obey their parents (Eph. 6:1), we shouldn't idolize and hold a picture of "family utopia" in our minds. We are called to serve God and others, not ourselves. Although a relationship with our parents is very important, Jesus wants us to have good relationships with Him and allow the cultivated soil of Christ-centered living be where the fruit of a godly relationships grows from.

Do we love God because He can fix the problems we have with our parents, or do we love God for Himself, because of what He's done for us and for Who He is? Do we love Him in the good times and hate Him in the bad times? Jesus picked up His cross, carried it to Calvary, and died a terrible death for our sakes. Are we willing to bear our burdens for *His* sake?

"He who finds his life will lose it, and he who loses his life for My sake will find it." Matthew 10:39

"Nevertheless I have this against you, that you have left your first love [for Christ]." Revelations 2:4

God is giving us the amazing and magnificent. He died the criminal's death that we justly deserved, bore the cross for the sake of the whole world on the way to Calvary, and then, He simply asks us to bear *our crosses* for the sake of His kingdom, showing our love for Him and others in sacrificial ways (Mat. 16:24, 1 Jn. 4:19). After that command, He immediately promised that we would actually have more joy "losing our life" than "finding it." We will be happier doing what God wants us to do than what we want to do!

What a wonderful God to do so much for us and then give us above and beyond what we justly deserve! What a God of mercy, kindness, and unending forgiveness! Thinking about Calvary should cause our hearts to ache with desire to see Jesus glorified. He is *so worthy* of it!

The Makeshift Memorial

(Continued from the beginning of the book.)

Sue had just received a letter from her friend Violet challenging her to purposefully honor her parents for one week. At first reluctantly, and then with heart, she took on the challenge. As the week went on, Sue purposed to try to show her parents respect in every way she could. Soon, she started realizing something very similar to what Violet had learned. The trying moments in their relationship were not all her parents' fault. She saw things in her life that needed improvement and worked at them. Over the next couple weeks, Sue talked to Violet, and as a result, started working on forgiving her parents when they offended her, being content with her parents' decisions, and overlooking the annoying ways they acted. She even tried to honor them when it seemed like they were causing a whole mess of problems. That was a huge step for her!

The relationship Sue shared with her parents got better. Eventually, Sue decided she had something that she thought she should confess to them. Although Sue had stopped running off to places she wasn't allowed to go behind her parents' back, she still felt like she should tell her parents what she had been doing. She hoped that she would not get into too much trouble, but she still knew that she would have to be completely honest.

"Hey Mom, Dad, can I talk with you for a minute?" Sue asked nervously. Remembering the last conversation she had similar to this one, she continued, "Um...I just wanted to let you know that I have been hanging out with Kelly at the mall without an adult. I lied about Margret being there..."

"WHAT!!" roared her Dad angrily, "You mean you have been going all these weeks without an adult! You could have been kidnapped! I can't believe it. How much do we do to protect you from danger? And smack...you go right on and do the dangerous stuff behind our backs! Do you think we have any reason at all for the rules we set in place for you?"

"Yeah... but I stopped and I am trying to make it right now." The conversation dragged on and on. Sue lost her temper again and it became a loud argument.

Not long after the conversation ended, Sue ran up to her room, frustrated. "I tried so hard but I am just failing. I can never please my parents. I won't ever make them happy. Maybe I should stop trying."

After a few minutes of crying, Sue looked up and noticed her Bible sitting on her desk. She had been reading on and off over the past several weeks because of Violet's suggestion. Picking it up, she sat on the floor near her bed and opened up to Romans, "For what I am doing, I do not understand. For what I will to do, that I do not practice; but what I hate, that I do" (Rom. 7:15).

"That's sure is a funny verse," Sue thought, half laughing. "It reminds me of how much I hate failing in the area of anger. I hate my temper, but I keep getting upset and dishonoring my parents." Sue sighed and continued reading.

A few verses later, Sue stumbled upon another verse that stood out to her: "O wretched man that I am! Who will deliver me from this body of death? I thank God – through Jesus Christ our Lord!" (Rom. 7:24-25a)

"'O wretched man...'" Sue read out loud. "'...who will deliver me? I thank God - through Jesus Christ our Lord!'"

That verse really made her think. "'Through Jesus Christ our Lord...'" Sue said again, meditatively. "Wow! Maybe Christ can help me with this relationship!"

Quickly forgetting this last thought, Sue raised herself from the floor, pulled Violet's last letter from her desk drawer, found Grandma's phone number included inside, and having

previously received permission to contact Grandma, dialed her number.

"Hello?" A sweet, shaky voice answered.

"Hi! My name is Sue. I'm Violet's friend."

"Oh! Hello dear, I've heard about you from Violet! You seem to be a good friend. A little firecracker, as I've heard. How can I help you today?"

"Well...um...Violet has been telling me about her conversations with you and how you've been encouraging her to have a better relationship with her parents. She challenged me to do the same, so I started trying, and it's really hard. I don't know what I'm doing wrong! I've done everything she's told me to do (sigh)! I have a feeling I'm leaving something out."

"Girl, I think I know what your problem is!" Grandma said emphatically. "I was a young lady once upon a time, so take it from me. You're probably missing out on a lot and leaving the icing off the cake!"

"Excuse me?"

"Sue, dear. Have you forgotten Jesus? Have you prayed recently?"

"Um...no."

"You should! He has invited you to! Let me see," she pondered while flipping through her Bible, "Was it Psalm 55:22, or was it...oh yes, here it is. It says, 'Cast your burden on the Lord, and He shall sustain you; He shall never permit the righteous to be moved.' Jesus wants to bear your burdens. If you bear your own burdens, you will get discouraged, but if you focus on what God has for you, there is much joy and freedom to be had!"

"That is what I want!" Sue cried, half-excitedly. "I would really like to have joy...and freedom."

"Yes. Life is wonderful. Believe me, I've lived eighty-nine years of it! Everything from a bird's song to a breathtaking sunrise reminds me of how blessed I am to know the Creator God personally. Throughout my life, His blessings have always been the most bountiful when I've trusted Him, enjoying the steadfastness of His love and keeping my life surrendered to Him. The real victory is for those who surrender."

"Maybe that's what I need to do, then. I feel like I could surrender to something. It would probably be better to surrender to God than to my old ways again." Sue said, half laughing.

"Absolutely, Sue. You're on the right track. I'm so proud of you! Could you call me back later today? I want to talk to you, but I have a doctor's appointment in thirty minutes."

"Oh, sure. I'll call you back."

"I will be praying for you, my friend! Stay strong!"

"Ok, bye!"

Sue hung up the phone and sat on her bed in deep thought. Looking up, Sue saw a piece of white material lying on the floor. It was a rag she had used to dust her room earlier that day. With the excitement of a sudden idea, she sprung from her bed, grabbed the rag, and ran out the door. Outside in the woods, she found a nice stick to which she attached the piece of white cloth.

"This will have to do." Sue thought, waving the makeshift flag in the air.

As the sun set behind the trees, Sue knelt to make an important choice before the Lord. As she stuck her flag into the ground, she prayed, "Here I am, God. My life is yours. The whole thing. *I* can't fix this relationship I have with my parents. *I* can't bridge this big empty gap that's formed between us over time. *I* can't fix my stinky attitudes. Only *you* can do it through me. I know you want the best for me, and I trust you. You alone are worthy of my heart and my life because You died for me. Jesus, I surrender all."

(Please read the conclusion.)

Conclusion

If you have gotten anything out of reading this book, I hope that you have been encouraged to pursue a deeper relationship with the Lord. I would have to say that as I started earnestly seeking the Lord in my personal life, it helped my family relationships tremendously!

Secondly, I hope that you have learned some things about your parents that you didn't know before and have been encouraged, at least in some way, about the relationships you share with them!

Perfectly Imperfect

I am definitely not a perfect child. Perhaps that's a good thing, because if I was, I probably wouldn't know what to say in this book! I struggle on a day-to-day basis. It is so easy for us to assume that we need to become a "certain way" before we can "have good relationships," etc. We agonize and groan then become discouraged because we haven't hit the mark. But, can we on our own?

The Bible says that "...all have sinned..." (Romans 3:23). The amazing thing is that this imperfection of ours qualifies us for God's *perfect* salvation. Through this, we can rejoice in our weaknesses, knowing that where we are weak, God can be strong in us (2 Cor. 12:9-10). God's strength is so much stronger than we could ever imagine. The more we realize we are incapable of living a godly life, the more we are able to allow God to step in and to be our Righteousness.

"In His days Judah will be saved, and Israel will dwell safely; now this is His name by which He will be called: THE LORD OUR RIGHTEOUSNESS." Jeremiah 23:6

Salvation

If you haven't already, I strongly encourage you to consider the gift of God's Son for salvation. I know that this book is full of references and inferences to following Christ, life in Christ, and so on. These thoughts won't help you any if you haven't realized what Christ can do for you, that He wants to offer you salvation from sin and hell (Mat. 13:49-50) and give you everlasting life with Him in heaven and abundant life with Him here on earth (Jn. 10:10). If you haven't received this gift that Jesus offers, it is absolutely a gift *worth opening.*

First, you must understand that your sin is detestable in the sight of God and turn away from it to receive God's gift of salvation and His power for living a godly life.

"For the wages of sin is death, but the **gift of God is eternal life** in Christ Jesus our Lord." Romans 6:23

You cannot just do this privately. If you are serious about this, let people know and get connected with other believers.

"...if you confess with your mouth the Lord Jesus and believe in your heart that God has raised Him from the dead, **you will be saved**. For with the heart one believes unto righteousness, and with the mouth confession is made unto salvation." Romans 10:9-10

Do not hesitate to call on God to show Himself to you. Ask Him for a sign that He is real. Know that whatever your past has been - good or bad - He is still more than willing to make you His child if you accept Him into your life.

"Therefore **He is also able to save to the uttermost** those who come to God through Him, since He always lives to make intercession for them." Hebrews 7:25

Read your Bible and pray daily. Seek to establish a living relationship with the living God. Expect that as you do so, you will start to change from the inside out.

"**I will give you a new heart** and put a new spirit within you; I will take the heart of stone out of your flesh and give you a heart of flesh. **I will put My Spirit within you** and cause you to walk in My statues, and you will keep My judgments and do them." Ezekiel 36:26-27

It would be good to make this a point of remembrance in your life and record something like the following in a place where you will be reminded of it in the future:

I, _____ _____, on this day of _____ gave my life to Jesus Christ, to follow Him, to learn from Him, to make Him Lord, and to serve from Him from now to the rest of eternity.

Appendix 1 The One Week of Honor Challenge

Below are many ways to show your parents appreciation, but this advice won't do anything for you unless you make honor the <u>reason</u> you do these things. Your desire to honor them will show by your obedience. Refrain from talking back, arguing, thinking and speaking negatively, and complaining. If you mess up in these areas during this week, don't feel too bad, just learn from your mistakes and try to do better next time! If it helps, you can make a copy of the challenge and check off the boxes as you go along. Enjoy!

Day 1: Sunday

- ☐ Set a timer and pray for your parents for 5 minutes.
- ☐ Think of all the positive things your parents have done for you in the past week, write them down, and thank your parents for them (even seemingly small things, like driving you places, making dinner, going to work, etc.). Try to think of at least ten.

Day 2: Monday

- ☐ Set a timer and pray for your parents for 5 minutes.
- ☐ Ask your parents what things make them feel the most loved, appreciated, and respected.
- ☐ Be sure to say "Good morning," "Good night," and "I love you" to your parents today.

Day 3: Tuesday

- ☐ Set a timer and pray for your parents for 5 minutes.
- ☐ Devise a special way to answer their phone calls, such as "Hello, this is the happy daughter/son of _____. How can I help you today?" This is especially fun when you are answering to the parent the greeting was intended to honor. If they call in today, use it!

Day 4: Wednesday

- ☐ Set a timer and pray for your parents for 5 minutes.
- ☐ Use your understanding of what makes your parents feel loved (which you learned on Monday) to do something they'd appreciate.

Day 5: Thursday

- ☐ Set a timer and pray for your parents for 5 minutes.
- ☐ Lend a helping hand. (Ideas: do something that's not your chore, help your parent carry in a briefcase or lunch bag from work, or offer to play with a sibling.)

Day 6: Friday

- ☐ Set a timer and pray for your parents for 5 minutes.
- ☐ If there is anything your parents have asked you to do that you haven't done yet, do it! If you've already done everything they want you to do, make a point to tell them about your week and ask about how their week was.

Day 7: Saturday

- ☐ Set a timer and pray for your parents for 5 minutes.
- ☐ Hide some notes of appreciation for your parents in places they'll stumble across (like on their computer, under their pillow, on the microwave, in their lunch, on a door, etc.).

Appendix 2 Creative Ways to Show Honor to Your Parents

Fun Ways to Show Your Parents that You Care about Them

(Taken from Chapter Two)

Answer the phone lovingly: When you know that your parent is calling in, say something sweet to make them feel special, like, "Hello, this is the happy daughter of Robert Normoyle! How may I help you?"

Practice spontaneous acts of kindness: Do something to relieve their burden when they don't know you're doing it! Listen for things they want done...the windows washed, the garage swept, trash taken out? Just washing or putting away dishes one night without being asked would be a blessing! Don't expect to be found out or look forward to praise or reward. Let the mere fact that you were able to be a blessing bless you in return.

Offer a shoulder massage: Ask your parents if they'd like a massage...some people (dads especially!) *really* appreciate this!

Develop thoughtful habits: Some examples might be a hug and kiss before bed or a warm after-work "Welcome home!" Other habits might include the simple and enthusiastic "please" and "thank you" or apologizing sincerely when you've wronged them.

Allow time for your parents to be alone: This might mean simply being quiet for them, cleaning something, or making dinner so they're not as busy. If you're old enough, you could babysit so that they can go out.

Give when they'd expect it least: Parents know that children like to give them gifts on Mother's Day or Christmas, but why not surprise them with a small gift "just because"? It could be a love note, a bouquet of wild-picked flowers, or even a picture you drew. It doesn't have to be big and you can be as creative as you want. The point is to let them know that you care!

Use sticky notes: When no one is around, pull out some sticky notes, write encouraging notes on them, and hide them around the house in places you know your family members will find.

Relationship To-Dos

(*Taken from Chapter 4*)

Make use of uplifting words. Amazing, spectacular, incredible, outstanding, fabulous...wow! What an encouraging family of words! "Mom, you did a spectacular job making dinner tonight! Thanks for your effort!!" "Dad, you are an incredible baseball player! Thanks for coming out to play with me!" How else can you make us of uplifting words in your life?

Make certain words and expressions taboo. If you have any discouraging expressions, stop using them! There's no need to discourage those around you, especially the parents who love and care for you. Your goal should be to encourage others and build them up (1 Thes. 5:11). Discouraging or dishonoring words and expressions might be "annoying," "stupid," "dumb," "Whaaaat?!?!," "Duuh," "Huh?" etc. Discouraging thoughts can also be portrayed in facial expressions, so watch out!

Respond Promptly. If Mom calls "Timmy!!", his response should be "Yes, Mom?" *immediately*. If you can, go to your parent when they call you so you can have eye contact with them as they speak. Even if you know *beyond a shadow of a doubt* that that particular call means that your mom is going to ask you to set the table for the fifth night in a row, go and help *joyfully* anyway. Your parents want to know that you're listening to them and that you care about them and what they have to say. Honor that! It's worth their relationship.

Ask good questions. When your parents are explaining something to you, don't just stand there and mumble, "Uh huh, uh huh..." while twirling your hair. Ask questions to help you understand what they're saying better and to help them know that you understand what you're being told. It might be good to say something like, "So, this is what I heard: you want me to mop the hallway, clean the toilets, and practice my multiplication flash cards, right?"

Other good questions to ask while your parents are giving instructions might be: "What time do you want this done by?" or "Is there anything else on your list?" Good questions are always respectful and never come out like, "Do I *have* to do that noooowww?" People come up with good questions when they're listening to the person talking and meanwhile planning how they can do what they're being told.

After the task is carried out, it's always good to report back to your parents and let them know you're done. They will want to know how well you did it, too, so be prepared to give account! Also, ask permission to be excused from the task when you are done so you don't leave them feeling like you've only done the job half-way. This attitude of responsibility helps the parent feel loved and valued.

Take note of their advice and wishes. Often children and parents experience tension over a conflict of particular interest. Perhaps it's the music you listen to, the friends you hang out with, the clothes you wear, or the movies you watch. Listen to your parents and make the changes necessary to honor them in full. If you want to go the extra mile, you can make them feel especially appreciated by asking them for advice on what you should wear, listen to, who to hang out with, etc. Do you already know what they're going to say? It's probably because they've been trying to get you to do something for a while. Break the tension today and obey!

Smile. Make your parents feel loved and appreciated – smile a big, award-winning, ear-to-ear, loving grin to make them feel special!

Appendix 3   Battlefield Tips

(Taken from chapter 6)

Most of the battle takes place in the mind and heart, so it's important to fill those places with God's truth! Here are some hints:

- *Pick a verse to think about each day.* Write it on a 3X5 card and carry it around so that you can pull it out to read as necessary. You could also write a verse on a sticky note and put it somewhere you can see it throughout the day. "For the word of God is living and powerful, and sharper than any two-edged sword..." Hebrews 4:12

- *Replace worldly music with uplifting music with a Christ-centered message.* What is your music like? Does it encourage you to live for God? Does is lead your spirit into worship, or does it encourage you to think or act selfishly? "Let the words of my mouth and the meditation of my heart be acceptable in Your sight, O Lord, my strength and my Redeemer." Psalm 19:14

- *Watch your influences.* Are the characters you watch on the television good or bad influences in your life? Do they honor their parents? Could you be picking up bad habits or attitudes from them?

- *Choose friends wisely.* Scripture infers that we will become like those we are around. We want to find wise friends so that we can become wise with them (See Prov. 13:20 and Prov. 12:26).

- *Pray about everything you do and about every concern you have.* "Rejoice always, pray without ceasing, in everything give thanks; for this is the will of God in

Christ Jesus for you" (1 Thess. 5:16-18). "Therefore humble yourselves under the mighty hand of God...casting all your care upon Him, for He cares for you" (1 Pet. 5:6-7).

- *Claim power over the enemy.* Because we are in Christ and Christ is in us, we have authority over evil in Jesus' name. Pray against evil and trust God for strength. "Be sober, be vigilant; because your adversary the devil walks about like a roaring lion, seeking whom he may devour. Resist him, steadfast in faith..." (1 Pet. 5:8-9a).

- *Find a prayer partner to support you in battle.* Wouldn't it be awful if every soldier had to slay his giants single-handedly? It may sound valiant, but in reality, it is actually <u>more valiant</u>, more challenging, <u>more encouraging</u> for the body of Christ, <u>and better</u> for you when you are transparent about your struggles with others. "Confess your trespasses to one another, and pray for one another, that you may be healed. The effective, fervent prayer of a righteous man avails much" (Jas 5:16).

- *Take every thought captive.* "...bringing every thought into captivity to the obedience of Christ" (2 Cor. 10:5).

- *Know that God wants to show you how strong <u>He is</u>, not how strong <u>you</u> can be.* Much of spiritual victory is actually surrender to Christ. "'Not by might nor by power, but by My Spirit' says the Lord of hosts" (Zech. 4:6b).

- *Remember that* **the battle is the Lord's**! "For the battle is the Lord's..." (1 Sam. 17:47b).

- *Praise the Lord that He has already won the war!* Although we still have small battles to fight, God has already won the war. Let's fight with Him! "Having disarmed principalities and powers, He made a public spectacle of them, *triumphing* over them in it" (Col. 2:15).

The Quick List – 20 Ways to Honor

1. Enthusiastically introduce them to others you know.
2. Enjoy being with them in public.
3. Thank them with gifts of appreciation and notes of encouragement.
4. Gracefully provide information for family decisions.
5. Praise them in front of others.
6. Deflect praise to them. When you are praised, thank the one who praised you, then deflect the honor to your parents for the ways they have helped you become who you are today.
7. Welcome their correction!
8. Thank them for the seemingly small and "expected" things they do, such as buying groceries, fixing a meal, fixing a faucet or a car, driving you around, etc. Think about how they spend their time on the things that indirectly benefit you and thank them for it.
9. Commit to honor your father and mother for your whole life.
10. Be under their authority.
11. Maintain a clear conscience with them.
12. Avoid even small things that dishonor your parents, such as being mindful of their pet peeves and not complaining.
13. Honor them in little ways, such as smiling, showing gratefulness, or praying for them.
14. Ask them for counsel.
15. Listen to them.
16. Purpose to be loyal to your parents and love them no matter what.
17. Share the details of your life and day with them.
18. Enjoy them – be proud of them and find joy in spending time with them.
19. Care for them in old age!
20. Honor their memory. Even after a parent passes away, his or her wise teachings and good example can be carried on for generations to come.

Appendix 4 Conversation Starters

Caution: Please avoid conversations you think might irritate them.

- [ ] Could you tell me about what it was like when you grew up?
- [ ] What was your hometown like?
- [ ] What was the economy like?
- [ ] How were your relationships with your parents?
- [ ] What were some of your favorite things to do?
- [ ] What are your dreams for my future?
- [ ] Do you have any fears about raising children? If so, what are they?
- [ ] If there was one thing you wanted me to know before I left home, what would it be?
- [ ] If you could know the answer to any question about me right now, what would it be?
- [ ] How can I help you?
- [ ] Is there any way I have wronged you and have not apologized or made it right again?
- [ ] On a scale of one to ten, how would you rate your relationship with me?
- [ ] What makes you feel loved?
- [ ] How can I be praying for you?

Conversation Starters to Use With Siblings

- [ ] What do you want to be when you grow up?
- [ ] What type of person do you want to become five years from now? (Both in respect to character and occupation.)
- [ ] Is there anything you want to do with me?
- [ ] Is there any way I have hurt you and not apologized for it?
- [ ] Do you feel encouraged by me?
- [ ] What things do I do that you enjoy?
- [ ] What makes you feel loved and special?
- [ ] How can I be praying for you?

Family Appreciation Game
-Courtesy of the Burnett family

Ideas on how to use this:

- Write each phrase (see below) on a piece of paper and ask your parents to write answers that relate to you
- Answer these questions on a piece of paper for your mom and dad and give it to them for encouragement
- Write these questions on index cards one question per card. Put them in a hat and make one person "it" and have everyone else pick a question and read the answer to the "it" person. Start another round with a new person and fresh cards until all players have been able to be "it."
- Hand them out to your siblings and answer the questions for Father's Day, Mother's Day, or a birthday.

You make me laugh when you:

You inspire me by your:

I appreciate:

You encourage me by:

I admire your:

You are super good at/with:

Without you:

You make me smile when:

I couldn't do without your:

One thing I like best about you:

Appendix 5 Let Them Know

Here is an example of something you could write to your parents if you want to let them know you want to honor them more. Keep in mind that you may need to modify it for yourself and your situation.

Dear Mom and/or Dad,

I have made a decision to live my life in a way that would please both you and the Lord Jesus from the inside out. Could you please let me know when I'm not respecting you and pray for me through this journey? I know I will need your support! I don't know what I'd do without you.

I'm sorry for all the times I have not obeyed or respected you properly. It has been wrong of me to treat you in those ways. I would really like to grow in these areas! I know you will help me grow, as you always have.

Thanks for caring for me! I love you both...

Sincerely,

_____

Resources

Family

-*Making Brothers and Sisters Best Friends* ~ Sarah, Stephen, and Grace Mally

-*Listening for Heaven's Sake* ~ Dr. Gary Sweeten, Dave Ping, and Anne Clippard

-Solvefamilyproblems.org (DVDs and CDs perinate to family issues)

-Lamplighter.net (Building Christ-like Character...One Story at a Time)

Following Christ

-*Victory in Christ* ~ Charles Trumbull

-*The Purpose Driven Life* ~ Rick Warren

-*For God, It's All about Relationship* ~ Daphne Chick

-*My Heart- Christ's Home* ~ Robert Boyd Munger

-*Absolute Surrender & Humility* ~ Andrew Murray

-*The Pilgrim's Progress* ~ John Bunyan (a story allegory)

-*Hinds' Feet on High Places* ~ Hannah Hurnard (a story allegory)

Sharing the Gospel

-*Will Our Generation Speak? A Call to be Bold with the Gospel* ~ Grace Mally

-*Out of the Salt Shaker and into the World* ~ Becky Pipper

-*Livingwaters.com* (Inspiring and Equipping Christians in Fulfilling the Great Commission)

Made in the USA
Middletown, DE
20 February 2020